GOODSON MUMBA

EFFECTIVE LEADERSHIP, EFFICIENT RESULTS

Navigating Success in the Modern Workplace

Copyright © 2024 by Goodson Mumba

All rights reserved. No part of this publication may be reproduced, stored or transmitted in any form or by any means, electronic, mechanical, photocopying, recording, scanning, or otherwise without written permission from the publisher. It is illegal to copy this book, post it to a website, or distribute it by any other means without permission.

First edition

ISBN: 9798335777063

This book was professionally typeset on Reedsy. Find out more at reedsy.com

Contents

Preface v
Acknowledgement vii
Dedication viii
Disclaimer ix

1 Chapter One: Introduction to Effective Leadership 1
2 Chapter Two: Visionary Leadership 12
3 Chapter Three: Strategic Decision Making 23
4 Chapter Four: Effective Communication 36
5 Chapter Five: Building High-Perfoming Teams 48
6 Chapter Six: Leading Through Change 60
7 Chapter Seven: Cultivating a Culture of Innovation 72
8 Chapter Eight: Leading with Emotional Intelligence 84
9 Chapter Nine: Optimizing Time Management and Productivity 96
10 Chapter Ten: Creating a Culture of Accountability 108
11 Chapter Eleven: Leading Remote and Distributed Teams 120
12 Chapter Twelve: Conflict Resolution and Negotiation Skills 132
13 Chapter Thirteen: Ethical Leadership and Corporate... 144
14 Chapter Fourteen: Strategies for Personal and Professional... 154
15 Chapter Fifteen: Sustaining Leadership Excellence 165

About the Author

Preface

In today's fast-paced and ever-evolving world, the role of leadership has never been more crucial. As organizations navigate the complexities of the modern workplace, the need for effective leadership that can drive efficiency and achieve results has become paramount. It is within this context that "Effective Leadership, Efficient Results: Navigating Success in the Modern Workplace" emerges—a comprehensive guide crafted to equip leaders with the knowledge, skills, and strategies necessary to thrive in today's dynamic landscape.

This book is born out of a deep understanding of the challenges and opportunities facing leaders in the modern workplace. Drawing upon extensive research, real-world experiences, and timeless principles of leadership, it offers a roadmap for success that is both practical and actionable. From cultivating a leadership mindset to mastering the art of communication, from building high-performing teams to leading through change, each chapter is meticulously crafted to provide insights, tools, and techniques that can be applied immediately to drive meaningful results.

But this book is more than just a collection of strategies and tactics—it is a call to action for leaders to embrace their role as agents of change and stewards of excellence. It challenges them to lead with integrity, empathy, and vision, to inspire others to greatness, and to leave a lasting legacy that transcends the boundaries of time and space.

As you embark on this journey through the pages of "Effective Leadership, Efficient Results," I invite you to approach it with an open mind and a willingness to learn. Whether you are a seasoned executive or an emerging leader, there is something within these pages for you—a nugget of wisdom, a spark of inspiration, a roadmap to success.

May this book serve as a guiding light on your leadership journey, empowering you to navigate the complexities of the modern workplace with confidence, clarity, and purpose. Together, let us unlock the potential of effective leadership and achieve efficient results that propel us towards a brighter future.

Warm regards,
Goodson Mumba

Acknowledgement

I would like to eternally and gratefully acknowledge the Almighty God for the infinite intelligence from His universal mind where we draw from all that we come to know and are yet to know. May I also acknowledge and thank everyone that has played a part in my journey of life in terms of spiritual, moral, emotional and material support.

Dedication

I extend my sincerest gratitude to my beloved wife, Edith Mumba, and our children, Angelina, Lubuto, Letticia, Lulumbi, and Butusho, for their unwavering support and understanding throughout the conception, writing, and eventual publication of this book, despite the sacrifices and challenges they endured.

Disclaimer

This book is a work of fiction. Names, characters, businesses, places, events, and incidents are either the products of the author's imagination or used in a fictitious manner. Any resemblance to actual persons, living or dead, or actual events is purely coincidental.

1

Chapter One: Introduction to Effective Leadership

"The Catalyst: Daniel's Awakening"

As the sun rose over the city skyline, Daniel Bennett, CEO of a once-thriving tech company, sat alone in his corner office, surrounded by towering stacks of reports and a sense of unease gnawing at him. The relentless pace of the modern workplace had taken its toll, and Daniel couldn't shake the feeling that something was amiss.

Lost in thought, Daniel's attention was suddenly drawn to a new arrival on his cluttered desk—a sleek, leather-bound book titled "Effective Leadership, Efficient Results: Navigating Success in the Modern Workplace." Curiosity piqued, Daniel flipped through its pages, his eyes scanning the bolded headings and insightful anecdotes within.

As he delved deeper, Daniel felt a spark of recognition ignite within him. The words on the page seemed to echo his own experiences—the struggle to balance ambition with authenticity, the quest for clarity in a sea of complexity, and the unyielding pressure to deliver results in an ever-evolving landscape.

With each turn of the page, Daniel found himself captivated by the book's wisdom, drawn to its promise of a new approach to leadership—one rooted in effectiveness and efficiency, rather than mere tradition or hierarchy. It was a revelation, a guiding light illuminating the path forward in an uncertain world.

Determined to heed the book's message, Daniel made a decision then and there—to embark on a journey of transformation, both for himself and for his company. With renewed purpose, he set out to share his newfound insights with his executive team, igniting a spark of inspiration that would soon spread throughout the organization.

Little did Daniel know, this pivotal moment would mark the beginning of a profound shift—a shift towards a new era of leadership excellence, where effectiveness and efficiency would reign supreme, and success would be measured not just in profits, but in the impact made on the lives of those they served.

Understanding the Role of Leadership in Achieving Organizational Goals "The Visionary's Call"

As Daniel immersed himself deeper into the teachings of "Effective Leadership, Efficient Results," a newfound clarity began to emerge—a clarity that would reshape his understanding of leadership and its pivotal role in achieving organizational goals.

Gathered around the polished mahogany table in the boardroom, Daniel's executive team listened intently as he shared his revelations from the book. With a sense of urgency in his voice, Daniel articulated the fundamental truth he had come to realize: that leadership was not just about giving orders or managing tasks, but about inspiring others to greatness and guiding them towards a shared vision.

Drawing upon the book's insights, Daniel painted a vivid picture of the future—a future where their company stood at the forefront of innovation, where every employee felt empowered to contribute their best, and where success was measured not just in profits, but in the positive impact they made on the world.

As he spoke, Daniel could see the spark of inspiration igniting in the eyes of his team, each member beginning to grasp the transformative power of effective leadership. Together, they embarked on a journey to define a bold new vision for the company—one that would propel them towards greatness and unite them in a common purpose.

With a renewed sense of purpose and determination, Daniel and his team set out to align their organizational goals with their shared vision, breaking down silos, fostering collaboration, and empowering every employee to contribute their unique talents towards a common goal.

Little did they know, this pivotal moment would mark the beginning of a remarkable journey—a journey fueled by the power of visionary leadership, where every challenge was met with courage, every setback with resilience, and every success with humble gratitude.

And as they forged ahead into the unknown, guided by the principles of effective leadership, they knew that their greatest achievements lay not in the destination, but in the journey itself—a journey filled with possibility, potential, and the promise of a brighter tomorrow.

Defining Effective Leadership Traits and Characters

"The Portrait of a Leader"

In the dimly lit conference room, Daniel stood before his executive team, a sense of anticipation hanging in the air as they delved into the next subpoint of their journey: defining effective leadership traits and characteristics.

With a projector casting a soft glow on the screen behind him, Daniel began to paint a vivid portrait of the qualities that distinguished true leaders from mere managers. Drawing upon the teachings of "Effective Leadership, Efficient Results," he spoke of integrity, empathy, and a relentless commitment to excellence as the cornerstones of effective leadership.

As he spoke, images flashed across the screen—scenes of leaders past and present, each embodying the virtues he described. From visionary pioneers who dared to dream big and challenge the status quo, to compassionate mentors who uplifted those around them with words of encouragement and acts of kindness, the tapestry of leadership unfolded before their eyes.

But it was not just the grand gestures or larger-than-life personas that defined effective leadership, Daniel emphasized. It was the small, everyday actions—the willingness to listen, the courage to admit mistakes, and the humility to seek guidance—that truly set great leaders apart.

With each trait and characteristic outlined, Daniel encouraged his team to reflect on their own leadership styles and identify areas for growth and development. Together, they engaged in lively discussions, sharing stories of past successes and failures, and challenging each other to strive for greatness in all they did.

And as the meeting drew to a close, Daniel couldn't help but feel a sense of pride and optimism wash over him. For in defining the traits of effective leadership, they had taken the first step towards becoming the leaders their company—and their world—needed them to be.

Little did they know, the journey ahead would be long and challenging, filled with obstacles and uncertainties. But armed with the knowledge and insight gleaned from their study of effective leadership, they were ready to face whatever lay ahead, united in their commitment to lead with integrity, empathy, and a relentless pursuit of excellence.

The Evolution of Leadership Theories

"Charting the Course: A Journey Through Leadership History"

As the afternoon sun filtered through the windows of the boardroom, Daniel and his executive team embarked on the next leg of their exploration into effective leadership: the evolution of leadership theories.

With a sense of reverence for the past and a keen eye on the future, Daniel began to guide his team through a chronological journey, tracing the lineage of leadership from its ancient roots to its modern-day manifestations.

As images of ancient philosophers and tribal chieftains flickered on the screen before them, Daniel spoke of the earliest theories of leadership—of the divine right of kings and the notion that leadership was bestowed upon a chosen few by the gods themselves.

But as societies evolved and civilizations flourished, so too did the theories of leadership. From the autocratic rule of emperors and dictators to the democratic ideals of the Enlightenment, each era brought with it new perspectives and insights into what it meant to lead.

As the slideshow progressed, Daniel paused to highlight key milestones in the evolution of leadership theory—the rise of scientific management in the Industrial Revolution, the emergence of trait theory in the early 20th century, and the groundbreaking work of behavioral psychologists like Kurt Lewin and Douglas McGregor.

But it was the dawn of the Information Age that truly revolutionized the way we think about leadership, Daniel explained. With the advent of globalization, technological innovation, and the democratization of knowledge, leaders were forced to adapt to an increasingly complex and interconnected world.

Drawing upon the teachings of "Effective Leadership, Efficient Results," Daniel challenged his team to think critically about how these historical perspectives could inform their approach to leadership in the modern workplace. How could they reconcile the lessons of the past with the demands of the present? And how could they leverage these insights to chart a course towards a brighter future?

As the discussion unfolded, Daniel couldn't help but feel a sense of awe at the vast tapestry of human experience laid out before them. For in understanding the evolution of leadership theories, they had unlocked a treasure trove of wisdom—a roadmap to guide them on their journey towards becoming the leaders their company—and their world—so desperately needed.

CHAPTER ONE: INTRODUCTION TO EFFECTIVE LEADERSHIP

Assessing Your Leadership Style:

"Reflections of Leadership: A Journey Within"

As the evening shadows lengthened, casting a soft glow over the boardroom, Daniel and his executive team delved into the next subpoint of their exploration into effective leadership: assessing their own leadership styles.

Seated around the polished oak table, each member of the team was handed a questionnaire—a series of probing inquiries designed to uncover their strengths, weaknesses, and inherent leadership tendencies. With pens poised and minds open, they embarked on a journey of self-discovery, guided by the principles outlined in "Effective Leadership, Efficient Results."

As the minutes ticked by, Daniel watched intently as his team grappled with the questions before them. Some hesitated, unsure of how to answer, while others dove in headfirst, eager to uncover the hidden truths lurking within.

With gentle encouragement and probing questions, Daniel guided his team through the process, offering insights and reflections gleaned from his own journey of self-assessment. Together, they explored the nuances of leadership—of the delicate balance between assertiveness and empathy, confidence and humility, vision and execution.

But it was not just the questionnaire that revealed their leadership styles, Daniel explained. It was the everyday interactions, the subtle gestures, and the way they carried themselves in moments of triumph and adversity alike. True leadership, he emphasized, was not something that could be measured by a single test or assessment—it was a journey of continuous growth and self-improvement.

As the session drew to a close, Daniel invited his team to share their insights and reflections, fostering a sense of openness and vulnerability within the group. For in embracing their strengths and acknowledging their weaknesses, they were taking the first step towards becoming the leaders they aspired to be.

And as they left the boardroom that evening, hearts and minds brimming with newfound awareness and understanding, Daniel couldn't help but feel a sense of optimism for the journey ahead. For in assessing their leadership styles, they had unlocked the door to a world of possibilities—a world where effectiveness and efficiency reigned supreme, and success was within reach for those bold enough to seize it.

Importance of Adaptability in Leadership:

"Embracing the Winds of Change"

As twilight descended upon the city, casting long shadows across the boardroom, Daniel and his executive team delved into the final subpoint of their exploration into effective leadership: the importance of adaptability.

Gathered around the table, Daniel began to speak of the ever-shifting landscape of the modern workplace—of the rapid pace of technological innovation, the emergence of new market trends, and the unpredictable twists and turns of global events. In such turbulent times, he explained, the ability to adapt and evolve was not just a luxury, but a necessity for survival.

Drawing upon the lessons of "Effective Leadership, Efficient Results," Daniel shared stories of leaders who had faced adversity with courage and resilience—of companies that had weathered storms, adapted to change, and emerged stronger than ever before.

But adaptability was not just about reacting to change, Daniel emphasized. It was about anticipating it, preparing for it, and embracing it as an opportunity for growth and transformation. It was about fostering a culture of innovation and agility within the organization, where every member felt empowered to challenge the status quo and explore new possibilities.

With each word, Daniel could see the spark of understanding igniting in the eyes of his team. For in the face of uncertainty, they recognized the power of adaptability to not only survive, but thrive in the modern workplace.

And as the meeting drew to a close, Daniel issued a challenge to his team—a challenge to embrace change with open arms, to learn from their mistakes, and to never lose sight of the vision that had brought them together in the first place.

For in the end, he knew, it was not the strongest or the smartest who would survive, but those who were most adaptable to change. And with that realization, Daniel and his team embarked on their journey towards a future filled with endless possibilities—a future where adaptability was not just a skill, but a way of life.

Cultivating a Leadership mindset

"Seeds of Leadership: Cultivating a Mindset of Growth"

As the moon rose high in the night sky, casting a soft glow through the windows of the boardroom, Daniel and his executive team delved into the final subpoint of their exploration into effective leadership: cultivating a leadership mindset.

With a sense of purpose and determination, Daniel began to speak of the power of mindset—the belief that one's abilities and qualities were not fixed, but could be developed and cultivated over time. It was a concept he had encountered in "Effective Leadership, Efficient Results," and one that resonated deeply with him as he reflected on his own journey as a leader.

Drawing upon personal anecdotes and insights from the book, Daniel shared stories of resilience and perseverance—of leaders who had faced seemingly insurmountable challenges and emerged stronger on the other side. It was not their natural talents or innate abilities that had carried them through, he explained, but their mindset—their unwavering belief in their own potential and their commitment to continuous growth and improvement.

But cultivating a leadership mindset was not just about positive thinking, Daniel emphasized. It was about embracing failure as a learning opportunity, seeking out feedback and mentorship, and maintaining a sense of curiosity and humility in the face of uncertainty.

With each word, Daniel could see the transformation taking place within his team. For in the darkness of the night, they were planting the seeds of leadership—a mindset of growth and possibility that would take root and flourish in the days and weeks to come.

And as the meeting drew to a close, Daniel issued a challenge to his team—a challenge to embrace their potential as leaders, to cultivate a mindset of growth and resilience, and to never lose sight of the vision that had brought them together.

For in the end, he knew, it was not the circumstances they faced or the obstacles in their path that would determine their success, but the mindset with which they approached them.

And with that realization, Daniel and his team embarked on their journey towards becoming the leaders they were destined to be—guided by the principles of effective leadership, and fueled by a mindset of growth and possibility.

2

Chapter Two: Visionary Leadership

"Beyond the Horizon: The Visionary's Quest"

As the first light of dawn painted the sky in hues of pink and gold, Daniel stood atop the rooftop terrace of his company's headquarters, gazing out over the sprawling city below. In his heart burned a fire—a fire ignited by the vision that had taken root within him, driving him forward with unwavering determination and purpose.

With each passing day, Daniel's resolve to lead his company towards greatness only grew stronger, fueled by the teachings of "Effective Leadership, Efficient Results." And so, as the sun began its ascent into the sky, Daniel gathered his executive team for a meeting unlike any other—a meeting dedicated to the power of visionary leadership.

Seated around the table in the boardroom, Daniel spoke with passion and conviction, painting a vivid picture of the future he envisioned for their company—a future where innovation knew no bounds, where every employee felt empowered to contribute their best, and where success was measured not just in profits, but in the positive impact they made on the world.

With each word, Daniel's vision took shape before their eyes—a bold and audacious plan to revolutionize their industry, to disrupt the status quo, and to leave a lasting legacy that would endure for generations to come.

But visionary leadership was not just about dreaming big, Daniel explained. It was about translating those dreams into action—about setting clear goals and objectives, and rallying the team around a common purpose. It was about fostering a culture of innovation and risk-taking, where failure was not feared, but embraced as a necessary step on the path to greatness.

As the meeting drew to a close, Daniel could see the spark of inspiration igniting in the eyes of his team. For in his vision, they saw not just the promise of a brighter future, but the opportunity to be a part of something truly extraordinary—a journey that would challenge them, inspire them, and ultimately, lead them to greatness.

And as they left the boardroom that day, hearts and minds brimming with possibility, Daniel knew that their journey had only just begun. For in the realm of visionary leadership, the horizon stretched endlessly before them—a vast and uncharted landscape, waiting to be explored by those bold enough to dare to dream.

Creating a Compelling Vision for the Organization:

"The Tapestry of Tomorrow: Weaving the Vision"

As the sun dipped below the horizon, casting long shadows across the boardroom, Daniel and his executive team delved deeper into the subpoint of visionary leadership: creating a compelling vision for the organization.

Seated around the table, the team listened intently as Daniel painted a vivid picture of the future—a future where their company stood as a beacon of innovation and excellence, where every employee felt inspired to unleash their full potential, and where their products and services transformed the lives of millions around the globe.

With passion and conviction in his voice, Daniel wove together the threads of his vision, each word resonating with the power of possibility. He spoke of breakthrough technologies yet to be invented, of markets yet to be conquered, and of a legacy yet to be written.

But a compelling vision was not just about lofty ideals and grandiose dreams, Daniel explained. It was about grounding those aspirations in reality—about identifying the key objectives and milestones that would guide their journey forward, and rallying the team around a shared purpose.

With each word, Daniel's vision began to take shape before their eyes—a roadmap to greatness, carefully crafted and meticulously planned. And as the team absorbed the magnitude of what lay before them, a sense of excitement and anticipation filled the room.

But creating a compelling vision was not just about words on a page, Daniel emphasized. It was about instilling a sense of ownership and accountability within the organization— empowering every employee to see themselves as stewards of the vision, and to play an active role in bringing it to life.

And as the meeting drew to a close, Daniel issued a challenge to his team—a challenge to embrace the vision with open hearts and open minds, and to channel their collective energy and passion towards its realization.

For in the end, he knew, their success would not be measured by the strength of their ideas alone, but by their ability to turn those ideas into reality—to weave the tapestry of tomorrow, one thread at a time. And with that realization, Daniel and his team embarked on their journey towards greatness, guided by the power of a compelling vision and fueled by the promise of a brighter future.

Communicating the Vision Effectively:

"The Symphony of Tomorrow: Harmonizing the Vision"

As twilight descended upon the city, casting long shadows across the boardroom, Daniel and his executive team continued their exploration of visionary leadership, delving into the subpoint of communicating the vision effectively.

Seated around the table, the team leaned in attentively as Daniel spoke with clarity and purpose, emphasizing the importance of articulating their shared vision in a way that resonated with every member of the organization.

Drawing upon the principles of "Effective Leadership, Efficient Results," Daniel spoke of the need to craft a compelling narrative—one that captured the hearts and minds of their employees and inspired them to action. It was not enough to simply outline the goals and objectives of the vision, he explained. They must breathe life into it, infusing it with passion and conviction that would ignite a fire in the hearts of all who heard it.

With each word, Daniel painted a vivid picture of the future they envisioned—a future where their company stood at the forefront of innovation, where every employee felt valued and empowered, and where their collective efforts made a meaningful impact on the world.

But communicating the vision effectively was not just about words, Daniel emphasized. It was about embodying the vision in everything they did—leading by example, living their values, and demonstrating their unwavering commitment to its realization.

With a sense of purpose and determination, Daniel challenged his team to become ambassadors of the vision—to share it with passion and enthusiasm, to inspire others to join them on their journey, and to empower every member of the organization to see themselves as integral to its success.

And as the meeting drew to a close, Daniel could feel a sense of excitement building within the room. For in the symphony of tomorrow, they had found their song—a melody of hope and possibility that would guide them on their journey towards greatness.

And with that realization, Daniel and his team set out to share their vision with the world—to spread its message far and wide, and to inspire others to join them in building a future filled with promise and potential.

Aligning Goals and Objectives with the Vision:

"Forging the Path: Aligning Dreams with Reality"

As the stars twinkled in the night sky, casting a soft glow over the boardroom, Daniel and his executive team delved into the critical subpoint of visionary leadership: aligning goals and objectives with the shared vision.

Seated around the table, the team leaned in with anticipation as Daniel spoke with clarity and conviction, emphasizing the importance of ensuring that every goal and objective they set was in perfect harmony with the overarching vision for the organization.

Drawing upon the teachings of "Effective Leadership, Efficient Results," Daniel spoke of the need to translate their lofty aspirations into tangible actions—to break down the vision into clear and actionable goals that would guide their journey forward.

With each word, Daniel outlined a roadmap to greatness—a series of strategic objectives designed to propel them towards their ultimate destination. From expanding into new markets to investing in research and development, each goal was carefully calibrated to bring them one step closer to realizing their vision.

But aligning goals and objectives with the vision was not just about setting targets and deadlines, Daniel emphasized. It was about fostering a culture of accountability and ownership within the organization—empowering every employee to see themselves as stakeholders in the journey towards greatness, and to take ownership of their role in achieving the vision.

With a sense of purpose and determination, Daniel challenged his team to become architects of the future—to align their individual goals and objectives with the overarching vision, and to work together towards a common purpose.

And as the meeting drew to a close, Daniel could feel a sense of unity and purpose permeating the room. For in aligning their goals and objectives with the vision, they had taken the first step towards transforming their dreams into reality—a journey filled with challenges, yes, but also with endless opportunities for growth and success.

And with that realization, Daniel and his team set out to forge the path ahead—to chart a course towards greatness, guided by the power of a shared vision and fueled by their unwavering commitment to its realization.

Empowering Teams to Work Towards the Vision:

"Empowering the Dreamers: Unleashing the Potential Within"

As the morning sun filtered through the windows of the boardroom, casting a warm glow over the table, Daniel and his executive team delved into the vital subpoint of visionary leadership: empowering teams to work towards the shared vision.

Seated around the table, the team listened intently as Daniel spoke with passion and purpose, emphasizing the importance of creating an environment where every employee felt empowered to contribute their best towards the realization of the vision.

Drawing upon the principles of "Effective Leadership, Efficient Results," Daniel spoke of the need to trust in the capabilities of their teams—to recognize and nurture the unique talents and perspectives that each member brought to the table.

With each word, Daniel painted a picture of a workplace where creativity flourished, where innovation thrived, and where every voice was valued and heard. It was not enough to simply set goals and objectives, he explained. They must empower their teams to take ownership of their work, to think outside the box, and to push the boundaries of what was possible.

But empowering teams was not just about giving them the freedom to innovate, Daniel emphasized. It was also about providing the support and resources they needed to succeed—whether through training and development opportunities, access to cutting-edge technology, or a culture of collaboration and teamwork.

With a sense of purpose and determination, Daniel challenged his team to become champions of empowerment—to lead by example, to inspire trust and confidence in their teams, and to create a culture where everyone felt empowered to make a difference.

And as the meeting drew to a close, Daniel could feel a sense of excitement building within the room. For in empowering their teams to work towards the shared vision, they had unlocked a wellspring of potential—a reservoir of creativity, innovation, and passion that would propel them towards greatness.

And with that realization, Daniel and his team set out to unleash the power of their teams—to harness the collective energy and enthusiasm of their employees, and to transform their shared vision into a reality that surpassed even their wildest dreams.

Overcoming Challenges in Vision Implementation:

"Navigating the Storm: A Test of Resilience"

As the sky darkened with ominous clouds, casting a somber tone over the boardroom, Daniel and his executive team faced the daunting subpoint of visionary leadership: overcoming challenges in vision implementation.

Seated around the table, tension hung heavy in the air as Daniel addressed the team, his voice steady despite the weight of the task ahead. He spoke of the inevitable obstacles and hurdles they would encounter on their journey towards realizing their shared vision—the doubts, the setbacks, and the unforeseen challenges that threatened to derail their progress.

Drawing upon the teachings of "Effective Leadership, Efficient Results," Daniel spoke of the need for resilience in the face of adversity—the courage to persevere in the darkest of times, and the unwavering belief in their ability to overcome any obstacle that stood in their way.

With each word, Daniel reminded his team of the strength that lay within them—the resilience that had carried them through past trials and tribulations, and the collective resolve to weather any storm that threatened to tear them apart.

But overcoming challenges in vision implementation was not just about sheer determination, Daniel emphasized. It was also about adaptability and flexibility—about being willing to pivot and adjust their approach in response to changing circumstances, and to learn from their failures as much as their successes.

With a sense of unity and purpose, Daniel challenged his team to face the challenges ahead with courage and resilience—to see them not as roadblocks, but as opportunities for growth and learning, and to emerge from each trial stronger and more determined than before.

And as the meeting drew to a close, Daniel could sense a newfound sense of determination within the room. For in the face of adversity, they had found strength in each other—a bond that would carry them through even the darkest of times, and propel them towards a future filled with hope and possibility.

And with that realization, Daniel and his team set out to navigate the storm ahead—to confront their challenges head-on, and to emerge victorious on the other side, stronger and more resilient than ever before.

Measuring Progress Towards the Vision:

"Charting the Course: Tracking Progress Amidst the Storm"

As daylight began to fade, casting a soft glow through the windows of the boardroom, Daniel and his executive team faced the critical subpoint of visionary leadership: measuring progress towards the shared vision.

Seated around the table, the team's faces were etched with determination as Daniel addressed them, his voice steady despite the weight of the task ahead. He spoke of the importance of setting clear metrics and benchmarks to track their progress—the need to measure not just the destination, but the journey itself.

Drawing upon the principles of "Effective Leadership, Efficient Results," Daniel spoke of the need for transparency and accountability in their approach to measuring progress. It was not enough to simply set goals and objectives, he explained. They must also establish key performance indicators and regularly assess their performance against them to ensure they stayed on track.

With each word, Daniel outlined a framework for tracking progress—a series of metrics and milestones designed to gauge their success in achieving the vision they had set forth. From revenue growth to customer satisfaction, each indicator was carefully chosen to provide a comprehensive view of their progress towards greatness.

But measuring progress was not just about numbers on a spreadsheet, Daniel emphasized. It was also about capturing the intangible—the sense of momentum, the spirit of collaboration, and the collective sense of purpose that fueled their journey forward.

With a sense of purpose and determination, Daniel challenged his team to embrace accountability—to hold themselves and each other to the highest standards of excellence, and to take ownership of their role in achieving the vision.

And as the meeting drew to a close, Daniel could sense a renewed sense of focus within the room. For in measuring their progress towards the shared vision, they had unlocked a powerful tool for driving success—a compass to guide them through the storm and towards a future filled with promise and possibility.

And with that realization, Daniel and his team set out to chart their course forward—to track their progress with diligence and determination, and to celebrate each milestone achieved on their journey towards greatness.

3

Chapter Three: Strategic Decision Making

"Crossroads of Destiny: The Art of Strategic Decision Making"

As the sun rose on a new day, casting golden rays through the windows of the boardroom, Daniel and his executive team gathered to explore the next chapter of their journey: strategic decision making.

Seated around the table, anticipation hung in the air as Daniel addressed the team, his voice resonating with a sense of purpose and determination. He spoke of the critical role that strategic decision making played in steering their organization towards success—the need to navigate the complex landscape of opportunities and challenges with clarity, vision, and foresight.

Drawing upon the principles of "Effective Leadership, Efficient Results," Daniel spoke of the importance of gathering all available information, analyzing it thoroughly, and considering the potential consequences of each decision before them. It was not enough to rely on gut instinct or intuition, he explained. They must approach each decision with a deliberate and systematic approach, grounded in data and informed by their collective wisdom and experience.

With each word, Daniel outlined a framework for strategic decision making—a series of steps designed to guide them through the process with confidence and precision. From defining the problem at hand to evaluating alternative courses of action, each step was carefully calibrated to ensure they made choices that aligned with their overarching vision and goals.

But strategic decision making was not just about logic and analysis, Daniel emphasized. It was also about intuition and instinct—about trusting their gut when faced with uncertainty, and having the courage to take calculated risks when necessary.

With a sense of unity and purpose, Daniel challenged his team to embrace the responsibility of strategic decision making—to approach each choice with the gravity it deserved, and to always keep the best interests of the organization at heart.

And as the meeting drew to a close, Daniel could sense a newfound sense of confidence within the room. For in the crossroads of destiny, they had found the opportunity to shape their future—to make decisions that would chart the course of their organization for years to come, and to lead them towards a destiny filled with promise and possibility.

And with that realization, Daniel and his team set out to embrace the challenge of strategic decision making—to navigate the twists and turns of their journey with wisdom and courage, and to emerge victorious on the other side, stronger and more resilient than ever before.

Understanding the Importance of Strategic Decision Making

"The Keystone of Success: Embracing Strategic Decision Making"

As the morning light bathed the boardroom in a soft glow, Daniel and his executive team delved deeper into the subpoint of understanding the importance of strategic decision making.

Seated around the table, the team listened intently as Daniel spoke with conviction, emphasizing the pivotal role that strategic decision making played in shaping the destiny of their organization. He spoke of the countless decisions, both big and small, that had led them to this moment—the risks taken, the opportunities seized, and the challenges overcome.

Drawing upon the teachings of "Effective Leadership, Efficient Results," Daniel spoke of the importance of strategic decision making in navigating the complexities of the modern business landscape. It was not just about making choices in the heat of the moment, he explained. It was about thinking several steps ahead, anticipating potential outcomes, and choosing the path that would best align with their long-term vision and goals.

With each word, Daniel underscored the gravity of their responsibility as leaders—to make decisions that would not only drive short-term success, but also lay the foundation for sustainable growth and prosperity in the years to come.

But understanding the importance of strategic decision making was not just about recognizing its significance, Daniel emphasized. It was also about embracing it as a fundamental part of their leadership journey—embracing the uncertainty, the complexity, and the inherent risks that came with the territory.

With a sense of purpose and determination, Daniel challenged his team to rise to the occasion—to approach each decision with courage and clarity, and to never lose sight of the bigger picture. For in the keystone of strategic decision making, they held the power to shape their organization's destiny and forge a path towards greatness.

And as the meeting drew to a close, Daniel could feel a sense of empowerment filling the room. For in understanding the importance of strategic decision making, they had unlocked the key to their organization's success—a key that would guide them through the challenges ahead and open the door to a future filled with limitless possibilities.

And with that realization, Daniel and his team set out to embrace the journey ahead—to make decisions with wisdom and courage, and to lead their organization towards a destiny defined by vision, purpose, and relentless pursuit of excellence.

Gathering and Analyzing Data for Informed Decisions

CHAPTER THREE: STRATEGIC DECISION MAKING

"In the Crucible of Knowledge: Harnessing the Power of Data"

As the morning sun illuminated the boardroom, casting a warm glow over the polished table, Daniel and his executive team delved into the critical subpoint of gathering and analyzing data for informed decisions.

Seated around the table, the team leaned in with anticipation as Daniel addressed them, his voice resonating with a sense of purpose and determination. He spoke of the importance of harnessing the power of data to inform their decision-making process—the need to gather accurate, relevant information and analyze it with rigor and precision before making any strategic choices.

Drawing upon the principles of "Effective Leadership, Efficient Results," Daniel spoke of the myriad sources of data available to them—from market research and customer feedback to financial reports and industry trends. It was not enough to rely on intuition or anecdotal evidence, he explained. They must approach each decision with a scientific mindset, grounded in empirical data and objective analysis.

With each word, Daniel underscored the transformative potential of data-driven decision making—a potential to unlock insights, uncover hidden patterns, and reveal opportunities that might otherwise remain obscured. But gathering and analyzing data was not just about collecting numbers and statistics, Daniel emphasized. It was about interpreting them in context, drawing meaningful conclusions, and using those insights to drive action and create value.

With a sense of urgency and purpose, Daniel challenged his team to embrace the crucible of knowledge—to become voracious consumers of data, to question assumptions, and to challenge conventional wisdom at every turn. For in the crucible of knowledge, they held the key to unlocking the secrets of their success and forging a path towards greatness.

And as the meeting drew to a close, Daniel could sense a newfound sense of determination within the room. For in gathering and analyzing data for informed decisions, they had armed themselves with a powerful tool for driving success—a tool that would guide them through the complexities of the modern business landscape and illuminate the path towards a future filled with promise and possibility.

And with that realization, Daniel and his team set out to embrace the challenge ahead—to gather and analyze data with rigor and precision, and to harness its power to drive their organization towards greatness.

Balancing Short-term and Long-term Goals

"The Dance of Time: Harmonizing Present and Future"

As the sun began its descent towards the horizon, casting a warm glow over the city streets, Daniel and his executive team convened in a quaint café, departing from the confines of the boardroom to explore the subpoint of balancing short-term and long-term goals.

Seated around a rustic wooden table, the team exchanged knowing glances, their surroundings a departure from the sterile environment of the boardroom. Here, amidst the gentle hum of conversation and the aroma of freshly brewed coffee, they felt a sense of liberation—a freedom to explore ideas and perspectives unencumbered by the constraints of corporate formality.

Daniel, his voice echoing with warmth and sincerity, spoke of the delicate dance between short-term imperatives and long-term aspirations—the need to strike a balance between the demands of the present and the vision of the future. It was not enough to focus solely on immediate results or distant dreams, he explained. They must find a way to harmonize the two, weaving them together into a seamless tapestry of purpose and intent.

Drawing upon the teachings of "Effective Leadership, Efficient Results," Daniel spoke of the dangers of short-sightedness—of sacrificing long-term sustainability for short-term gains, and the pitfalls of becoming too fixated on distant horizons, losing sight of the opportunities that lay before them in the here and now.

With each word, Daniel emphasized the importance of maintaining a holistic perspective—a perspective that allowed them to navigate the complexities of time with wisdom and grace. But balancing short-term and long-term goals was not just about finding a compromise between competing interests, Daniel emphasized. It was about embracing the inherent tension between them, recognizing that each played a vital role in shaping their organization's destiny.

With a sense of camaraderie and shared purpose, Daniel challenged his team to embark on a journey of discovery—a journey that would take them beyond the confines of the present moment and into the realm of infinite possibility. For in the dance of time, they held the power to shape their future and create a legacy that would endure for generations to come.

And as the meeting drew to a close, Daniel and his team lingered in the café, savoring the warmth of the moment and the promise of what lay ahead. For in balancing short-term and long-term goals, they had unlocked the key to sustainable success—a key that would guide them through the twists and turns of their journey and lead them towards a future filled with boundless opportunity.

Involving Stakeholders in the Decision-Making Process

"Voices of Influence: Enriching Decision-Making Through Collaboration"

As the sun dipped below the skyline, casting a soft glow over the city streets, Daniel and his executive team gathered in a vibrant co-working space, departing from the traditional confines of the boardroom to explore the subpoint of involving stakeholders in the decision-making process.

Seated amidst the buzz of creativity and innovation, the team exchanged eager glances, invigorated by the energy of their surroundings. Here, surrounded by the hum of conversation and the eclectic décor, they felt a sense of openness and possibility—a freedom to engage with stakeholders in a more dynamic and inclusive manner.

Daniel, his voice resonating with sincerity and conviction, spoke of the transformative power of collaboration—the need to involve stakeholders from all levels of the organization in the decision-making process. It was not enough to rely solely on the insights of the executive team, he explained. They must harness the collective wisdom and experience of their employees, customers, and partners to inform their choices and drive their organization forward.

Drawing upon the principles of "Effective Leadership, Efficient Results," Daniel spoke of the importance of creating a culture of inclusivity and transparency—a culture where every voice was valued and heard, and where decisions were made with the input and buy-in of those most affected by them.

With each word, Daniel emphasized the richness that came from diverse perspectives and experiences. But involving stakeholders in the decision-making process was not just about seeking input for the sake of it, Daniel emphasized. It was about fostering genuine dialogue and collaboration, creating opportunities for meaningful engagement and empowering stakeholders to take ownership of the decisions that impacted them.

With a sense of purpose and determination, Daniel challenged his team to embrace the power of collective intelligence—to reach beyond the confines of the executive suite and tap into the wealth of knowledge and insight that existed within their organization and beyond.

And as the meeting drew to a close, Daniel and his team lingered in the co-working space, buoyed by the spirit of collaboration and shared purpose. For in involving stakeholders in the decision-making process, they had unlocked a wellspring of creativity and innovation—a resource that would guide them through the challenges ahead and lead them towards a future filled with boundless opportunity and growth.

Implementing Decision-Making Frameworks

"Frameworks of Action: Building the Path Forward"

As twilight descended upon the city, casting long shadows across the bustling streets, Daniel and his executive team convened in a modern innovation hub, departing from the conventional boardroom to explore the subpoint of implementing decision-making frameworks.

Surrounded by the vibrant energy of innovation, the team exchanged eager glances, invigorated by the dynamic atmosphere of their surroundings. Here, amidst the whir of creativity and the sleek, minimalist design, they felt a sense of possibility—a freedom to explore new approaches to decision-making that would propel their organization forward.

Daniel, his voice infused with determination and purpose, spoke of the need to establish clear frameworks for decision-making—the need to define the processes and procedures that would guide their choices and ensure alignment with their overarching goals and values. It was not enough to rely solely on intuition or ad hoc methods, he explained. They must establish a systematic approach that would foster consistency, accountability, and effectiveness in their decision-making.

Drawing upon the principles of "Effective Leadership, Efficient Results," Daniel spoke of the various decision-making frameworks available to them—from traditional models like SWOT analysis and cost-benefit analysis to more innovative approaches like design thinking and agile methodology. Each framework, he explained, offered its own unique advantages and could be tailored to suit the specific needs and challenges they faced as an organization.

With each word, Daniel emphasized the importance of flexibility and adaptability in their approach to decision-making frameworks. But implementing decision-making frameworks was not just about choosing the right tools, Daniel emphasized. It was about fostering a culture of learning and continuous improvement—a culture where experimentation was encouraged, and where failures were viewed not as setbacks, but as opportunities for growth and refinement.

With a sense of excitement and anticipation, Daniel challenged his team to embrace the journey of exploration—to experiment with different frameworks, to learn from their successes and failures, and to iterate and evolve their approach over time. For in the frameworks of action, they held the key to unlocking their organization's full potential and charting a course towards greatness.

And as the meeting drew to a close, Daniel and his team lingered in the innovation hub, inspired by the possibilities that lay before them. For in implementing decision-making frameworks, they had laid the groundwork for a future filled with innovation, agility, and success—a future where every choice was guided by clarity of purpose and fueled by the spirit of collaboration and continuous improvement.

Evaluating the Effectiveness of Decisions

"The Crucible of Reflection: Evaluating the Forge of Decision"

As the city lights twinkled like stars in the night sky, Daniel and his executive team gathered in a serene rooftop garden, departing from the conventional meeting spaces to explore the subpoint of evaluating the effectiveness of decisions.

Surrounded by the tranquility of nature, the team exchanged thoughtful glances, enveloped by the serenity of their surroundings. Here, amidst the rustle of leaves and the gentle breeze, they felt a sense of introspection—a freedom to reflect on the outcomes of their decisions and glean insights that would shape their future endeavors.

Daniel, his voice measured yet impassioned, spoke of the importance of reflection in the decision-making process—the need to pause, take stock, and assess the impact of their choices on their organization and its stakeholders. It was not enough to simply make decisions and move on, he explained. They must cultivate a culture of continuous learning and improvement, where every decision served as an opportunity for growth and refinement.

Drawing upon the principles of "Effective Leadership, Efficient Results," Daniel spoke of the various methods for evaluating the effectiveness of decisions—from quantitative metrics like return on investment and key performance indicators to qualitative assessments like stakeholder feedback and lessons learned reviews. Each method, he explained, offered its own unique insights and could be used to inform future decision-making and drive organizational success.

With each word, Daniel underscored the importance of humility and open-mindedness in their approach to evaluation.

But evaluating the effectiveness of decisions was not just about measuring outcomes, Daniel emphasized. It was also about embracing failure as a learning opportunity, recognizing that even the most well-intentioned decisions could yield unintended consequences, and being willing to course-correct and adapt in light of new information.

With a sense of resolve and determination, Daniel challenged his team to embrace the crucible of reflection—to engage in honest and transparent dialogue about their successes and failures, to learn from their experiences, and to use those insights to inform their future decisions.

And as the meeting drew to a close, Daniel and his team lingered in the rooftop garden, enveloped by the quiet beauty of the night. For in evaluating the effectiveness of decisions, they had unlocked a powerful tool for driving continuous improvement—a tool that would guide them through the uncertainties of the future and lead them towards a destiny defined by wisdom, resilience, and relentless pursuit of excellence.

4

Chapter Four: Effective Communication

"The Symphony of Connection: Mastering the Art of Effective Communication"

As dawn painted the sky in hues of pink and gold, Daniel and his executive team gathered in a historic library, their chosen sanctuary to explore the intricacies of effective communication.

Surrounded by towering shelves of wisdom and knowledge, the team exchanged knowing smiles, feeling a sense of reverence for the space that held the collective wisdom of generations. Here, amidst the hushed whispers of ancient tomes and the soft rustle of pages, they felt a deep appreciation for the power of words—a power that could inspire, unite, and transform.

Daniel, his voice imbued with warmth and sincerity, spoke of communication as the cornerstone of leadership—the bedrock upon which trust, collaboration, and success were built. It was

CHAPTER FOUR: EFFECTIVE COMMUNICATION

not enough to simply convey information, he explained. They must strive to connect on a deeper level—to engage hearts as well as minds, and to foster a sense of belonging and purpose within their organization.

Drawing upon the principles of "Effective Leadership, Efficient Results," Daniel spoke of the various facets of effective communication—from active listening and empathy to clarity and authenticity. Each facet, he explained, played a crucial role in building rapport, fostering understanding, and creating alignment among team members.

With each word, Daniel underscored the importance of intentionality and mindfulness in their communication practices. But effective communication was not just about the words they spoke, Daniel emphasized. It was also about the way they listened—the way they conveyed respect and empathy, and the way they created space for diverse perspectives to be heard and valued.

With a sense of reverence and purpose, Daniel challenged his team to embrace the art of communication—to strive for clarity and transparency in their messages, to cultivate empathy and understanding in their interactions, and to harness the power of storytelling to inspire and motivate those around them.

And as the meeting drew to a close, Daniel and his team lingered in the library, surrounded by the echoes of wisdom that filled the space. For in the symphony of connection, they had discovered the key to unlocking the full potential of their organization—a key that would open doors to innovation, collaboration, and success beyond measure.

Importance of Clear and Transparent Communication

"Clarity's Beacon: Illuminating the Path Forward"

As the morning sun filtered through stained-glass windows, casting vibrant patterns of light across the library's ancient wooden shelves, Daniel and his executive team delved deeper into the subpoint of the importance of clear and transparent communication.

Surrounded by the weight of centuries of knowledge, the team exchanged determined glances, their minds alight with the gravity of the topic at hand. Here, amidst the quiet reverence of the library, they felt a sense of urgency—a need to harness the power of clarity and transparency to navigate the complexities of their organization's journey.

Daniel, his voice a beacon of conviction and clarity, spoke of communication as the lifeblood of their organization—the thread that bound them together and guided them towards their shared goals. It was not enough to simply convey information, he explained. They must strive for absolute clarity in their messages, ensuring that every word was understood and every intention transparent.

Drawing upon the teachings of "Effective Leadership, Efficient Results," Daniel spoke of the transformative potential of clear and transparent communication—from fostering trust and credibility to enhancing collaboration and driving alignment. Each aspect, he emphasized, was essential to building a culture of openness and accountability within their organization.

With each word, Daniel underscored the importance of honesty and authenticity in their communication practices.

But clear and transparent communication was not just about what they said, Daniel emphasized. It was also about how they said it—the tone of their voice, the language they used, and the non-verbal cues they conveyed.

With a sense of purpose and determination, Daniel challenged his team to embrace clarity as their guiding light—to strive for simplicity and directness in their messages, to welcome feedback and questions, and to create an environment where transparency was not just a goal, but a way of life.

And as the meeting drew to a close, Daniel and his team basked in the warm glow of understanding that filled the library. For in the importance of clear and transparent communication, they had discovered a beacon to guide them through the uncertainties of the future—a beacon that would illuminate the path forward and lead them towards a destiny defined by clarity, trust, and unwavering commitment to excellence.

Active Listening Techniques for Leaders

"Echoes of Understanding: The Art of Active Listening"

As the afternoon sun bathed the library in a golden glow, Daniel and his executive team embarked on a journey into the subpoint of active listening techniques for leaders.

Surrounded by the timeless wisdom of the library's ancient tomes, the team leaned in with anticipation, ready to uncover the secrets of this essential leadership skill. Here, amidst the quiet reverence of the library, they felt a sense of openness—a willingness to embrace the transformative power of truly hearing and understanding one another.

Daniel, his voice gentle yet commanding, spoke of active listening as the cornerstone of effective communication—the bridge that connected leaders with their teams, fostering trust, empathy, and collaboration. It was not enough to simply hear the words of others, he explained. They must strive to truly listen—to tune in not only to what was being said, but also to the emotions, intentions, and unspoken messages beneath the surface.

Drawing upon the principles of "Effective Leadership, Efficient Results," Daniel spoke of the various techniques for active listening—from maintaining eye contact and nodding in acknowledgment to paraphrasing and reflecting back what had been said. Each technique, he emphasized, served to deepen understanding, build rapport, and strengthen relationships among team members.

With each word, Daniel underscored the importance of presence and empathy in their listening practices. But active listening was not just about the mechanics, Daniel emphasized. It was also about cultivating a mindset of curiosity and humility—a willingness to set aside preconceived notions and truly engage with the perspectives and experiences of others.

With a sense of humility and openness, Daniel challenged his team to embrace the art of active listening—to approach every interaction with a spirit of genuine curiosity and empathy, and to create space for every voice to be heard and valued.

And as the meeting drew to a close, Daniel and his team basked in the warmth of connection that filled the library. For in the echoes of understanding, they had discovered a powerful tool for building trust and fostering collaboration—a tool that would guide them towards a future defined by unity, empathy, and shared purpose.

Nonverbal Communication Skills

"The Language of Silence: Mastering Nonverbal Communication"

As twilight descended upon the library, casting long shadows across the aisles of books, Daniel and his executive team delved into the subpoint of nonverbal communication skills.

Surrounded by the hushed stillness of the library, the team leaned in with keen interest, eager to uncover the nuances of this silent language. Here, amidst the ancient wisdom of the written word, they felt a sense of reverence—a recognition of the power that lies within the unspoken gestures and expressions that convey so much more than words ever could.

Daniel, his voice soft yet commanding, spoke of nonverbal communication as the silent symphony that underpins every interaction—the subtle cues that reveal our true thoughts, feelings, and intentions. It was not enough to focus solely on what was said, he explained. They must also pay attention to the language of the body—the posture, gestures, and facial expressions that often speak volumes without uttering a single word.

Drawing upon the teachings of "Effective Leadership, Efficient Results," Daniel spoke of the various aspects of nonverbal communication—from maintaining open body language and making eye contact to mirroring and matching the demeanor of others. Each aspect, he emphasized, contributed to the overall effectiveness of their communication and played a crucial role in building trust and rapport with their teams.

With each word, Daniel underscored the importance of authenticity and mindfulness in their nonverbal communication practices. But nonverbal communication was not just about controlling their own body language, Daniel emphasized. It was also about being attuned to the nonverbal cues of others—to listen not only with their ears, but also with their eyes and hearts, and to respond with empathy and understanding.

With a sense of reverence and humility, Daniel challenged his team to embrace the language of silence—to harness the power of nonverbal communication to deepen connection, build trust, and foster collaboration among team members.

And as the meeting drew to a close, Daniel and his team sat in contemplative silence, surrounded by the whispers of the library's ancient tomes. For in mastering the language of silence, they had unlocked a powerful tool for leadership—a tool that would guide them towards a future defined by understanding, empathy, and authentic connection.

Providing Constructive Feedback

"The Forge of Growth: Nurturing Through Constructive Feedback"

As evening draped the library in shadows, Daniel and his executive team embarked on a journey into the subpoint of providing constructive feedback.

Surrounded by the timeless wisdom of the library's ancient tomes, the team leaned in with anticipation, ready to explore the delicate art of offering guidance and support. Here, amidst the quiet sanctuary of knowledge, they felt a sense of responsibility—a recognition of the role they played in nurturing the growth and development of their team members.

Daniel, his voice a blend of empathy and determination,

CHAPTER FOUR: EFFECTIVE COMMUNICATION

spoke of constructive feedback as the forge where greatness is forged—the crucible in which potential is honed and talent is refined. It was not enough to simply point out mistakes or shortcomings, he explained. They must strive to provide feedback that was both honest and compassionate, guiding their team members towards improvement while preserving their dignity and self-esteem.

Drawing upon the principles of "Effective Leadership, Efficient Results," Daniel spoke of the various elements of constructive feedback—from specificity and timeliness to empathy and encouragement. Each element, he emphasized, contributed to the overall effectiveness of their feedback and played a crucial role in fostering a culture of continuous learning and improvement within their organization.

With each word, Daniel underscored the importance of humility and empathy in their feedback practices. But providing constructive feedback was not just about offering criticism, Daniel emphasized. It was also about recognizing and celebrating the strengths and achievements of their team members, and acknowledging the progress they had made on their journey towards excellence.

With a sense of empathy and compassion, Daniel challenged his team to embrace the role of mentor and guide—to approach every feedback conversation with empathy and understanding, and to create a safe space for open and honest dialogue.

And as the meeting drew to a close, Daniel and his team sat in reflective silence, surrounded by the wisdom of the library's ancient tomes. For in providing constructive feedback, they had discovered a powerful tool for growth—a tool that would guide them towards a future defined by continuous learning, improvement, and collective achievement.

Handling Difficult Conversations

"Navigating the Rapids: Steadfast Amidst Difficult Conversations"

As night fell and the library's aisles were cast in shadows, Daniel and his executive team embarked on the challenging subpoint of handling difficult conversations.

Surrounded by the weight of centuries of knowledge, the team leaned in with somber determination, ready to confront the inevitable challenges that lay ahead. Here, amidst the quiet expanse of the library, they felt a sense of resolve—a recognition of the need to navigate the turbulent waters of disagreement and conflict with grace and resilience.

Daniel, his voice steady yet compassionate, spoke of difficult conversations as the crucible of growth—the arena in which trust is forged and relationships are strengthened. It was not enough to shy away from confrontation or to sweep issues under the rug, he explained. They must face difficult conversations head-on, with courage and integrity, in order to address conflicts, resolve misunderstandings, and foster deeper understanding and connection.

Drawing upon the teachings of "Effective Leadership, Efficient Results," Daniel spoke of the various strategies for handling difficult conversations—from active listening and empathy to assertiveness and problem-solving. Each strategy, he emphasized, served to create a safe and supportive environment for dialogue, where all parties felt heard, respected, and valued.

With each word, Daniel underscored the importance of emotional intelligence and resilience in their approach to difficult conversations. But handling difficult conversations was not just about the words they spoke, Daniel emphasized. It was also about the way they managed their emotions and remained steadfast in the face of adversity, staying true to their values and principles even in the midst of conflict.

With a sense of determination and solidarity, Daniel challenged his team to embrace difficult conversations as opportunities for growth—to approach them with humility and empathy, and to seek resolution with courage and compassion.

And as the meeting drew to a close, Daniel and his team sat in reflective silence, surrounded by the timeless wisdom of the library's ancient tomes. For in handling difficult conversations, they had discovered a source of strength and resilience—a source that would guide them through the challenges of the present and lead them towards a future defined by understanding, collaboration, and mutual respect.

Leveraging Technology for Communication Efficiency

"Bridging Beyond Borders: Uniting Through Technological Efficiency"

As the moon cast its gentle glow upon the library's tranquil surroundings, Daniel and his executive team delved into the subpoint of leveraging technology for communication efficiency.

Surrounded by the timeless wisdom contained within the library's ancient tomes, the team's anticipation was palpable as they prepared to explore the transformative potential of modern tools. Here, amidst the quiet reverence of knowledge, they felt a sense of excitement—a recognition of the boundless opportunities that awaited them in the realm of technological innovation.

Daniel, his voice infused with enthusiasm and vision, spoke of technology as the bridge that spanned the vast distances between team members, enabling seamless communication and collaboration across borders and time zones. It was not enough to rely solely on traditional methods of communication, he explained. They must harness the power of technology to streamline their workflows, enhance productivity, and foster greater connectivity among their distributed teams.

Drawing upon the principles of "Effective Leadership, Efficient Results," Daniel spoke of the various technologies available to them—from video conferencing and instant messaging to project management software and collaboration platforms. Each technology, he emphasized, offered its own unique advantages and could be tailored to suit the specific needs and challenges they faced as an organization.

With each word, Daniel underscored the importance of adaptability and innovation in their approach to leveraging technology. But technology was not just about efficiency, Daniel emphasized. It was also about fostering a sense of connection and belonging among team members, despite physical distance or time constraints.

With a sense of excitement and determination, Daniel challenged his team to embrace technology as a force for positive change—to explore new tools and platforms, to experiment with innovative solutions, and to create a virtual environment where every team member felt valued and empowered to contribute.

And as the meeting drew to a close, Daniel and his team sat in contemplative silence, surrounded by the quiet hum of the library's ancient tomes. For in leveraging technology for communication efficiency, they had discovered a pathway to unity and collaboration—a pathway that would bridge the gaps between them and lead them towards a future defined by innovation, connectivity, and shared success.

5

Chapter Five: Building High-Perfoming Teams

"Forging the Vanguard: Building High-Performing Teams"

As dawn broke and the first rays of sunlight spilled into the library, Daniel and his executive team gathered once more, their hearts set on exploring the intricacies of building high-performing teams.

Surrounded by the silent guardianship of the library's ancient tomes, the team's anticipation was palpable as they prepared to embark on this crucial chapter of their leadership journey. Here, amidst the timeless wisdom of the written word, they felt a sense of purpose—a recognition of the profound impact that effective teams could have on their organization's success.

Daniel, his voice resonant with passion and conviction, spoke of high-performing teams as the vanguard of organizational excellence—the driving force behind innovation, collaboration, and sustained success. It was not enough to simply assemble a group of talented individuals, he explained. They must cultivate an environment of trust, synergy, and shared purpose, where every team member felt valued and empowered to contribute their unique strengths and perspectives.

Drawing upon the principles of "Effective Leadership, Efficient Results," Daniel spoke of the various elements that constituted high-performing teams—from clear goals and roles to effective communication and collaboration. Each element, he emphasized, played a crucial role in fostering a culture of excellence and driving performance to new heights.

With each word, Daniel underscored the importance of diversity and inclusion in their approach to building teams. But high-performing teams were not just about achieving results, Daniel emphasized. They were also about fostering a sense of belonging and camaraderie among team members, where every voice was heard and every contribution valued.

With a sense of purpose and determination, Daniel challenged his team to embrace the journey of building high-performing teams—to cultivate an environment where trust and respect flourished, where innovation was celebrated, and where every team member felt inspired to reach their full potential.

And as the meeting drew to a close, Daniel and his team sat in contemplative silence, surrounded by the timeless wisdom of the library's ancient tomes. For in building high-performing teams, they had embarked on a journey of transformation—a journey that would lead them towards a future defined by unity, excellence, and collective achievement.

Understanding Team Dynamics

"Harmony in Motion: Unraveling the Tapestry of Team Dynamics"

As the morning sun continued to cast its golden light upon the library, Daniel and his executive team delved deeper into the subpoint of understanding team dynamics.

Surrounded by the quiet wisdom of the library's ancient tomes, the team leaned in with rapt attention, eager to unravel the intricate threads that wove together the fabric of their teams. Here, amidst the hallowed halls of knowledge, they felt a sense of reverence—a recognition of the complexities that lay beneath the surface of their collective endeavors.

Daniel, his voice filled with insight and empathy, spoke of team dynamics as the heartbeat of their organization—the rhythm that propelled their teams forward, driving collaboration, innovation, and success. It was not enough to simply assemble a group of talented individuals, he explained. They must strive to understand the unique dynamics at play within each team, recognizing the diverse personalities, skills, and perspectives that contributed to their collective identity.

Drawing upon the principles of "Effective Leadership, Efficient Results," Daniel spoke of the various factors that influenced team dynamics—from individual personalities and communication styles to team composition and leadership approach. Each factor, he emphasized, played a crucial role in shaping the interactions and relationships within their teams, and ultimately, their performance and effectiveness.

With each word, Daniel underscored the importance of empathy and observation in their approach to understanding team dynamics. But team dynamics were not just about surface-level interactions, Daniel emphasized. They were also about delving deeper, uncovering the underlying motivations, fears, and aspirations that drove their team members, and creating an environment where everyone felt seen, heard, and valued.

With a sense of curiosity and determination, Daniel challenged his team to embrace the complexity of team dynamics—to cultivate an environment where open dialogue and feedback were encouraged, where conflicts were addressed with empathy and respect, and where every team member felt empowered to contribute their unique talents and perspectives.

And as the meeting drew to a close, Daniel and his team sat in reflective silence, surrounded by the timeless wisdom of the library's ancient tomes. For in understanding team dynamics, they had unlocked the key to fostering synergy and collaboration—a key that would guide them towards a future defined by unity, cohesion, and collective achievement.

Establishing Trust and Psychological Safety

"Foundations of Trust: Cultivating Safety in the Crucible of Collaboration"

As the sun ascended higher in the sky, bathing the library in warm light, Daniel and his executive team delved further into the subpoint of establishing trust and psychological safety within their teams.

Surrounded by the timeless wisdom of the library's ancient tomes, the team leaned in with a sense of purpose, understanding the paramount importance of fostering an environment where trust and psychological safety thrived. Here, amidst the silent guardianship of knowledge, they felt a profound responsibility—a recognition of the pivotal role trust played in shaping the dynamics of their teams.

Daniel, his voice a blend of empathy and resolve, spoke of trust and psychological safety as the bedrock upon which effective teams were built—the crucible in which innovation, collaboration, and resilience flourished. It was not enough to simply mandate trust, he explained. They must cultivate an environment where every team member felt valued, respected, and empowered to share their ideas and take risks without fear of judgment or reprisal.

Drawing upon the principles of "Effective Leadership, Efficient Results," Daniel spoke of the various elements that contributed to trust and psychological safety—from transparent communication and vulnerability to accountability and empathy. Each element, he emphasized, played a crucial role in fostering a culture of openness, respect, and mutual support within their teams.

With each word, Daniel underscored the importance of authenticity and vulnerability in their approach to establishing trust and psychological safety. But trust was not just about words, Daniel emphasized. It was also about actions—consistently demonstrating integrity, fairness, and reliability in their interactions with team members, and creating a sense of belonging and shared purpose that transcended individual differences.

With a sense of determination and compassion, Daniel challenged his team to embrace the journey of cultivating trust and psychological safety—to lead by example, to listen with empathy, and to create space for every team member to contribute their unique perspectives and talents without fear of judgment or reprisal.

And as the meeting drew to a close, Daniel and his team

sat in reflective silence, surrounded by the quiet wisdom of the library's ancient tomes. For in establishing trust and psychological safety, they had laid the groundwork for a future defined by resilience, collaboration, and collective achievement—a future where every team member felt valued, respected, and empowered to reach their full potential.

Setting Clear Goals and Expectations

"Guiding Stars: Illuminating the Path with Clear Goals"

As the day progressed and the library hummed with the energy of discovery, Daniel and his executive team delved deeper into the subpoint of setting clear goals and expectations.

Surrounded by the quiet wisdom of the library's ancient tomes, the team leaned in with renewed focus, understanding the pivotal role that clear goals played in guiding their teams towards success. Here, amidst the hallowed halls of knowledge, they felt a sense of purpose—a recognition of the importance of providing their teams with a clear direction and purpose.

Daniel, his voice resonant with conviction and clarity, spoke of clear goals and expectations as the guiding stars that illuminated the path forward—the beacons that kept their teams focused, motivated, and aligned with their organizational objectives. It was not enough to simply have vague aspirations, he explained. They must define concrete, measurable goals that provided a roadmap for their teams to follow, and set clear expectations for performance and accountability.

Drawing upon the principles of "Effective Leadership, Efficient Results," Daniel spoke of the various elements that constituted clear goals and expectations—from specificity and measurability to relevance and time-bound deadlines. Each element, he emphasized, played a crucial role in ensuring that their teams understood what was expected of them and how their efforts contributed to the larger mission of the organization.

With each word, Daniel underscored the importance of communication and alignment in their approach to setting clear goals and expectations. But goals were not just about achieving results, Daniel emphasized. They were also about inspiring and motivating their teams, instilling a sense of purpose and meaning in their work, and creating a shared vision that united them in pursuit of common objectives.

With a sense of purpose and determination, Daniel challenged his team to embrace the discipline of goal-setting—to work collaboratively to define ambitious yet achievable goals, and to communicate them clearly and transparently to their teams.

And as the meeting drew to a close, Daniel and his team sat in contemplative silence, surrounded by the timeless wisdom of the library's ancient tomes. For in setting clear goals and expectations, they had laid the foundation for a future defined by focus, alignment, and collective achievement—a future where every team member understood their role and contribution to the organization's success, and worked together towards a common purpose.

Fostering Collaboration and Creativity

"Harmony of Minds: Cultivating Collaboration and Creativity"

As the library's serene atmosphere persisted, Daniel and his executive team delved into the subpoint of fostering collaboration and creativity.

Surrounded by the silent guardianship of the library's ancient tomes, the team leaned in with eager anticipation, recognizing the transformative potential of cultivating a culture where collaboration and creativity flourished. Here, amidst the sacred halls of knowledge, they felt a sense of inspiration—a recognition of the boundless possibilities that awaited them when minds came together in harmony.

Daniel, his voice infused with passion and vision, spoke of collaboration and creativity as the lifeblood of innovation—the catalysts that propelled their teams beyond the ordinary towards the extraordinary. It was not enough to simply work in silos or adhere to rigid structures, he explained. They must foster an environment where ideas flowed freely, where diverse perspectives were valued, and where every team member felt empowered to contribute their creativity and expertise.

Drawing upon the principles of "Effective Leadership, Efficient Results," Daniel spoke of the various elements that constituted fostering collaboration and creativity—from creating opportunities for cross-functional collaboration to encouraging experimentation and risk-taking. Each element, he emphasized, played a crucial role in unleashing the full potential of their teams and driving innovation and excellence.

With each word, Daniel underscored the importance of inclusivity and openness in their approach to fostering collaboration and creativity. But collaboration was not just about working together, Daniel emphasized. It was also about creating a culture of trust and respect, where every team member felt valued and supported, and where ideas were evaluated based on merit rather than hierarchy.

With a sense of excitement and determination, Daniel challenged his team to embrace the spirit of collaboration and creativity—to break down barriers, to embrace diversity of thought, and to create an environment where innovation thrived.

And as the meeting drew to a close, Daniel and his team sat in contemplative silence, surrounded by the timeless wisdom of the library's ancient tomes. For in fostering collaboration and creativity, they had unlocked the key to unlocking the full potential of their teams—a key that would guide them towards a future defined by innovation, excellence, and collective achievement.

Resolving Conflicts Within Teams

"Harmony in Dissonance: Navigating Conflict with Grace"

As daylight waned and shadows lengthened within the library, Daniel and his executive team delved into the crucial subpoint of resolving conflicts within teams.

Surrounded by the solemn presence of the library's ancient tomes, the team's demeanor shifted to one of solemnity, recognizing the inevitability of discord within their ranks. Here, amidst the hallowed halls of knowledge, they felt a sense of responsibility—a recognition of the need to confront conflicts head-on, with wisdom and compassion.

Daniel, his voice a steady beacon of reassurance and guidance, spoke of conflict resolution as the crucible in which unity and understanding were forged—the opportunity to transform discord into harmony, and dissent into growth. It was not enough to ignore or suppress conflicts, he explained. They must face them with courage and empathy, seeking resolution while preserving relationships and mutual respect.

Drawing upon the principles of "Effective Leadership, Efficient Results," Daniel spoke of the various strategies for resolving conflicts—from open dialogue and active listening to mediation and compromise. Each strategy, he emphasized, had its place in their toolkit for navigating the complexities of human interaction and fostering a culture of mutual understanding and collaboration.

With each word, Daniel underscored the importance of empathy and patience in their approach to conflict resolution. But conflict was not just about disagreement, Daniel emphasized. It was also an opportunity for growth and learning, a chance to gain deeper insight into the perspectives and motivations of their team members, and to strengthen relationships through honest and respectful dialogue.

With a sense of determination and humility, Daniel challenged his team to embrace the challenges of conflict resolution—to approach every disagreement with an open heart and mind, and to seek resolution with grace and compassion.

And as the meeting drew to a close, Daniel and his team sat in reflective silence, surrounded by the quiet wisdom of the library's ancient tomes. For in resolving conflicts within teams, they had discovered a pathway to greater unity and understanding—a pathway that would guide them towards a future defined by resilience, empathy, and collective achievement.

Recognizing and Rewarding Team Achievements

"Celebrating Success: Honoring the Tapestry of Team Achievements"

As the sun dipped below the horizon and the library was bathed in the soft glow of twilight, Daniel and his executive team delved into the subpoint of recognizing and rewarding team achievements.

Surrounded by the timeless wisdom of the library's ancient tomes, the team's spirits lifted with anticipation, understanding the significance of acknowledging the collective efforts that propelled their organization forward. Here, amidst the serene sanctum of knowledge, they felt a sense of gratitude—a recognition of the importance of celebrating milestones and successes along their journey.

Daniel, his voice brimming with warmth and appreciation, spoke of recognizing and rewarding team achievements as the glue that bound their teams together—the fuel that ignited their passion and dedication. It was not enough to simply acknowledge individual contributions, he explained. They must shine a spotlight on the collective achievements that resulted from collaboration, synergy, and shared vision.

Drawing upon the principles of "Effective Leadership, Efficient Results," Daniel spoke of the various ways to recognize and reward team achievements—from public praise and awards ceremonies to bonuses and career advancement opportunities. Each method, he emphasized, served to reinforce the importance of teamwork and inspire continued excellence

CHAPTER FIVE: BUILDING HIGH-PERFOMING TEAMS

among their teams.

With each word, Daniel underscored the importance of gratitude and generosity in their approach to recognizing and rewarding team achievements. But recognition was not just about tangible rewards, Daniel emphasized. It was also about creating a culture where every team member felt valued and appreciated, where their contributions were seen and acknowledged, and where success was celebrated as a collective triumph.

With a sense of joy and camaraderie, Daniel challenged his team to embrace the practice of recognizing and rewarding team achievements—to cultivate an environment where appreciation flowed freely, and where every milestone was an opportunity for celebration and reflection.

And as the meeting drew to a close, Daniel and his team sat in contented silence, surrounded by the quiet wisdom of the library's ancient tomes. For in recognizing and rewarding team achievements, they had discovered a source of motivation and inspiration—a source that would fuel their journey towards greater heights of success and fulfillment, together as one cohesive unit.

6

Chapter Six: Leading Through Change

"Navigating the Winds of Change: Leading Through Turbulent Seas"

As the library stood as a bastion of serenity, Daniel and his executive team turned their attention to the pivotal chapter on leading through change.

Surrounded by the weight of knowledge within the library's ancient tomes, the team prepared to embark on a journey through uncharted waters, where the only constant was the inevitability of change. Here, amidst the silent expanse of the library, they felt a sense of anticipation—a recognition of the challenges and opportunities that lay ahead.

Daniel, his voice a steady beacon of guidance and resilience, spoke of leading through change as the captain navigating a ship through stormy seas—the steadfast presence that guided their teams through uncertainty and adversity. It was not enough to merely weather the storms of change, he explained. They must chart a course that embraced transformation, leveraging change as an opportunity for growth and innovation.

Drawing upon the principles of "Effective Leadership, Efficient Results," Daniel spoke of the various facets of leading through change—from fostering a culture of adaptability and resilience to providing clear direction and communication during times of transition. Each facet, he emphasized, played a crucial role in guiding their teams through the complexities of change and emerging stronger on the other side.

With each word, Daniel underscored the importance of empathy and vision in their approach to leading through change. But leadership was not just about steering the ship, Daniel emphasized. It was also about inspiring confidence and trust in their teams, empowering them to embrace change with courage and optimism, and instilling a sense of purpose and direction amidst uncertainty.

With a sense of determination and resolve, Daniel challenged his team to embrace change as a catalyst for growth and transformation—to lead by example, to communicate openly and transparently, and to foster a culture where innovation and adaptability thrived.

And as the meeting drew to a close, Daniel and his team sat in contemplative silence, surrounded by the quiet wisdom of the library's ancient tomes. For in leading through change, they had embarked on a journey of discovery—a journey that would test their mettle and resilience, but ultimately lead them towards a future defined by progress, resilience, and collective achievement.

Understanding the Nature of Change in the Workplace

"Embracing the Tide: Unraveling the Essence of Workplace Change"

As the library's hallowed halls echoed with the resonance of knowledge, Daniel and his executive team delved deeper into the subpoint of understanding the nature of change in the workplace.

Surrounded by the ancient tomes that whispered tales of wisdom, the team leaned in with a sense of anticipation, recognizing the profound impact that change wielded in shaping the fabric of their organization. Here, amidst the sacred sanctuary of knowledge, they felt a sense of reverence—a recognition of the transformative power that awaited them as they unraveled the essence of workplace change.

Daniel, his voice resonant with insight and empathy, spoke of change as the ever-flowing tide—the relentless force that ebbed and flowed, shaping the landscape of their organization with each passing moment. It was not enough to merely react to change, he explained. They must strive to understand its essence, its motivations, and its implications, in order to navigate its currents with grace and resilience.

Drawing upon the principles of "Effective Leadership, Efficient Results," Daniel spoke of the various dimensions of workplace change—from technological advancements and market shifts to organizational restructuring and cultural evolution. Each dimension, he emphasized, carried its own unique challenges and opportunities, requiring a nuanced understanding and strategic approach to manage effectively.

With each word, Daniel underscored the importance of adaptability and foresight in their approach to understanding workplace change. But change was not just about adaptation,

Daniel emphasized. It was also about embracing the opportunities it presented, fostering a culture where innovation and growth flourished amidst uncertainty and upheaval.

With a sense of curiosity and determination, Daniel challenged his team to embrace change as a catalyst for progress and renewal—to approach it with an open mind and a willingness to learn, and to seek opportunities for innovation and adaptation in the face of adversity.

And as the meeting drew to a close, Daniel and his team sat in contemplative silence, surrounded by the timeless wisdom of the library's ancient tomes. For in understanding the nature of change in the workplace, they had unlocked a pathway to resilience and growth—a pathway that would guide them towards a future defined by agility, innovation, and collective achievement.

Communicating Change Effectively

"Sailing Through Stormy Seas: Mastering the Art of Effective Change Communication"

As the library's shadows danced in the flickering candlelight, Daniel and his executive team delved further into the subpoint of communicating change effectively.

Surrounded by the weight of centuries of knowledge within the library's ancient tomes, the team leaned in with a sense of purpose, understanding the pivotal role that communication played in guiding their organization through turbulent waters of change. Here, amidst the silent expanse of the library, they felt a sense of urgency—a recognition of the need to navigate the delicate balance of transparency and reassurance when communicating change.

Daniel, his voice a steady beacon amidst the storm, spoke of effective change communication as the compass that guided their teams through uncertainty—the lifeline that kept them anchored amidst the tempest of transition. It was not enough to simply announce changes and expect compliance, he explained. They must engage in open, honest, and empathetic communication that addressed fears, uncertainties, and doubts, while instilling confidence and clarity in the organization's direction.

Drawing upon the principles of "Effective Leadership, Efficient Results," Daniel spoke of the various elements of effective change communication—from crafting clear, consistent messages to actively listening to and addressing concerns from all stakeholders. Each element, he emphasized, played a crucial role in fostering trust, understanding, and alignment among their teams.

With each word, Daniel underscored the importance of empathy and transparency in their approach to communicating change. But effective communication was not just about words, Daniel emphasized. It was also about listening with compassion, acknowledging the emotions that accompanied change, and providing support and guidance to navigate the transition.

With a sense of empathy and determination, Daniel challenged his team to embrace the responsibility of effective change communication—to become stewards of clarity and reassurance, guiding their teams through the stormy seas of uncertainty with wisdom and compassion.

And as the meeting drew to a close, Daniel and his team sat in reflective silence, surrounded by the quiet wisdom of the library's ancient tomes. For in mastering the art of effective change communication, they had equipped themselves with a powerful tool—a tool that would guide them through the challenges of change and lead them towards a future defined by resilience, unity, and collective achievement.

Building Resilience in Yourself and Your Team

"Fortifying Foundations: Cultivating Resilience Amidst Change"

As the library's tranquil ambiance persisted, Daniel and his executive team delved into the vital subpoint of building resilience in oneself and one's team.

Surrounded by the wisdom enshrined within the library's ancient tomes, the team approached this topic with a sense of gravity, understanding the profound significance of resilience in navigating the turbulent seas of change. Here, amidst the sacred sanctum of knowledge, they felt a solemn reverence—a recognition of the fortitude required to weather the storms of transformation.

Daniel, his voice a steadfast beacon amidst uncertainty, spoke of resilience as the bedrock upon which their organization would rise from adversity—the unwavering strength that would carry them through even the darkest of times. It was not enough to simply endure change, he explained. They must cultivate resilience, both within themselves and within their teams, fostering a culture of adaptability, determination, and perseverance.

Drawing upon the principles of "Effective Leadership, Efficient Results," Daniel spoke of the various strategies for building resilience—from fostering a growth mindset and practicing self-care to providing support and encouragement to team members. Each strategy, he emphasized, served to bolster their collective ability to withstand the challenges that lay ahead.

With each word, Daniel underscored the importance of empathy and support in their approach to building resilience. But resilience was not just about individual strength, Daniel emphasized. It was also about fostering a sense of solidarity and camaraderie within their teams, creating a support network where team members could lean on each other in times of need and draw strength from their shared experiences.

With a sense of determination and unity, Daniel challenged his team to embrace the journey of building resilience—to cultivate inner strength and fortitude, and to empower their teams to face adversity with courage and resilience.

And as the meeting drew to a close, Daniel and his team sat in reflective silence, surrounded by the quiet wisdom of the library's ancient tomes. For in building resilience in themselves and their teams, they had equipped themselves with the resilience needed to navigate the challenges of change and emerge stronger, more united, and more resilient than ever before.

Anticipating and Addressing Resistance to Change

CHAPTER SIX: LEADING THROUGH CHANGE

"Navigating the Rapids: Addressing Resistance Amidst the Currents of Change"

As the library's hallowed halls echoed with the whispers of ages past, Daniel and his executive team delved into the crucial subpoint of anticipating and addressing resistance to change.

Surrounded by the weight of knowledge within the library's ancient tomes, the team approached this topic with a sense of solemnity, understanding the formidable obstacles that resistance could pose to their journey through change. Here, amidst the sacred sanctuary of knowledge, they felt a sense of urgency—a recognition of the need to navigate the treacherous currents of resistance with wisdom and resolve.

Daniel, his voice a steady beacon amidst the tumult, spoke of resistance as the rocks that threatened to dash their organization's ship against the shore—the obstacles that must be navigated with care and foresight. It was not enough to simply dismiss resistance or bulldoze through it, he explained. They must seek to understand its roots, address its concerns, and enlist its energy in service of the organization's goals.

Drawing upon the principles of "Effective Leadership, Efficient Results," Daniel spoke of the various strategies for anticipating and addressing resistance—from fostering open dialogue and transparency to providing support and education to those affected by change. Each strategy, he emphasized, served to disarm resistance and transform it into a catalyst for positive change.

With each word, Daniel underscored the importance of empathy and patience in their approach to addressing resistance. But resistance was not just about opposition, Daniel emphasized. It was also about fear, uncertainty, and loss—

emotions that must be acknowledged and addressed with compassion and understanding.

With a sense of determination and empathy, Daniel challenged his team to embrace the challenge of addressing resistance—to approach it with humility and curiosity, and to seek common ground and shared purpose amidst the turbulence of change.

And as the meeting drew to a close, Daniel and his team sat in contemplative silence, surrounded by the timeless wisdom of the library's ancient tomes. For in anticipating and addressing resistance to change, they had unlocked the key to navigating the rapids of uncertainty and emerging stronger, more united, and more resilient on the other side.

Providing Support During Transition Periods

"Anchors in the Storm: Providing Support Amidst Transition"

As the library's tranquil ambiance persisted, Daniel and his executive team turned their focus to the critical subpoint of providing support during transition periods.

Surrounded by the venerable tomes that held the collective wisdom of generations, the team approached this topic with a sense of compassion, understanding the upheaval and uncertainty that accompanied periods of change. Here, amidst the serene sanctuary of knowledge, they felt a solemn responsibility—a recognition of the need to offer solace and guidance to their team members navigating through turbulent waters.

Daniel, his voice a comforting presence amidst the storm, spoke of support as the lifeboat that carried their team members through rough seas—the reassuring presence that provided stability amidst chaos. It was not enough to simply announce changes and expect individuals to adapt on their own, he explained. They must extend a helping hand, offering guidance, reassurance, and resources to support their team members through the transition.

Drawing upon the principles of "Effective Leadership, Efficient Results," Daniel spoke of the various ways to provide support during transition periods—from offering training and skill development opportunities to providing emotional support and encouragement. Each method, he emphasized, served to alleviate the anxieties and uncertainties that arose during times of change, fostering a sense of resilience and confidence among their team members.

With each word, Daniel underscored the importance of empathy and solidarity in their approach to providing support. But support was not just about practical assistance, Daniel emphasized. It was also about creating a culture where every team member felt seen, heard, and valued—a culture of compassion and solidarity that extended beyond professional boundaries.

With a sense of compassion and determination, Daniel challenged his team to embrace the responsibility of providing support during transition periods—to be beacons of stability and guidance amidst uncertainty, and to foster a sense of belonging and resilience among their team members.

And as the meeting drew to a close, Daniel and his team sat in reflective silence, surrounded by the quiet wisdom of the library's ancient tomes. For in providing support during transition periods, they had become anchors in the storm—steady, reassuring presences that guided their team members through turbulent waters and towards calmer seas of stability and growth.

Learning from Past Change Initiatives

"Charting the Course: Navigating Change Through the Lens of Experience"

As the library's ambiance embraced them in its timeless embrace, Daniel and his executive team delved into the pivotal subpoint of learning from past change initiatives.

Surrounded by the weight of knowledge within the library's ancient tomes, the team approached this topic with a sense of introspection, understanding the invaluable lessons that lay hidden within the annals of their organization's history. Here, amidst the sacred sanctuary of knowledge, they felt a solemn reverence—a recognition of the wisdom waiting to be gleaned from the echoes of past experiences.

Daniel, his voice a steady beacon amidst the sea of history, spoke of learning from past change initiatives as the compass that guided their organization through uncharted waters—the map that illuminated the pitfalls and pathways of their journey. It was not enough to simply embark on new initiatives without reflection, he explained. They must study the successes and failures of the past, extracting valuable insights to inform their current and future endeavors.

Drawing upon the principles of "Effective Leadership, Efficient Results," Daniel spoke of the various dimensions of learning from past change initiatives—from conducting thorough post-mortems and root cause analyses to cultivating a culture of continuous improvement and adaptation. Each dimension, he emphasized, offered an opportunity to distill wisdom from experience, turning setbacks into stepping stones and triumphs into templates for success.

With each word, Daniel underscored the importance of humility and open-mindedness in their approach to learning from the past. But learning was not just about gathering data, Daniel emphasized. It was also about fostering a culture where mistakes were viewed as opportunities for growth, and where every team member felt empowered to contribute their insights and perspectives.

With a sense of reverence and determination, Daniel challenged his team to embrace the wisdom of the past—to approach each new change initiative with a spirit of curiosity and humility, and to draw upon the lessons of history to chart a course towards a brighter future.

And as the meeting drew to a close, Daniel and his team sat in contemplative silence, surrounded by the timeless wisdom of the library's ancient tomes. For in learning from past change initiatives, they had unlocked a reservoir of knowledge—a reservoir that would guide them through the challenges of change and towards a future defined by resilience, innovation, and collective achievement.

7

Chapter Seven: Cultivating a Culture of Innovation

"Seeds of Innovation: Cultivating a Garden of Creativity"

In the hallowed halls of the library, Daniel and his executive team embarked on the transformative journey outlined in chapter seven: cultivating a culture of innovation.

Surrounded by the quiet wisdom of ancient tomes, the team approached this chapter with a sense of anticipation, recognizing the potential for growth and renewal that lay within the fertile soil of innovation. Here, amidst the sacred sanctuary of knowledge, they felt a stirring of excitement—a recognition of the boundless possibilities awaiting them as they nurtured the seeds of creativity within their organization.

Daniel, his voice a symphony of inspiration and determination, spoke of innovation as the lifeblood that fueled their organization's evolution—the spark that ignited the flames of progress and transformation. It was not enough to simply embrace innovation as a buzzword, he explained. They must

CHAPTER SEVEN: CULTIVATING A CULTURE OF INNOVATION

cultivate a culture where creativity flourished, where every team member felt empowered to challenge the status quo, and where bold ideas were celebrated and nurtured.

Drawing upon the principles of "Effective Leadership, Efficient Results," Daniel spoke of the various elements that constituted a culture of innovation—from fostering a spirit of experimentation and risk-taking to providing the resources and support necessary for creative exploration. Each element, he emphasized, played a crucial role in creating an environment where innovation thrived.

With each word, Daniel underscored the importance of curiosity and collaboration in their approach to cultivating a culture of innovation. But innovation was not just about breakthrough ideas, Daniel emphasized. It was also about creating a culture where failure was viewed as a stepping stone to success, and where every setback was seen as an opportunity for growth and learning.

With a sense of excitement and determination, Daniel challenged his team to embrace the journey of innovation—to approach their work with a spirit of curiosity and experimentation, and to create an environment where creativity and innovation were valued and celebrated.

And as the meeting drew to a close, Daniel and his team sat in contemplative silence, surrounded by the timeless wisdom of the library's ancient tomes. For in cultivating a culture of innovation, they had planted the seeds of transformation—a garden of creativity that would blossom and flourish, guiding them towards a future defined by innovation, excellence, and collective achievement.

Creating an Environment Conducive to Innovation

"Nurturing Innovation: Crafting the Canvas for Creativity"

As the library's tranquil ambiance persisted, Daniel and his executive team delved further into the subpoint of creating an environment conducive to innovation.

Surrounded by the profound silence of ancient tomes, the team approached this topic with a sense of purpose, understanding the critical role that environment played in nurturing creativity. Here, amidst the serene sanctuary of knowledge, they felt a solemn responsibility—a recognition of the need to sculpt a space where innovation could take root and flourish.

Daniel, his voice a gentle melody amidst the stillness, spoke of creating an environment conducive to innovation as the artisan crafting a canvas for creativity—the architect designing the blueprint for innovation to thrive. It was not enough to simply expect innovation to emerge organically, he explained. They must intentionally cultivate an environment that fostered curiosity, experimentation, and collaboration.

Drawing upon the principles of "Effective Leadership, Efficient Results," Daniel spoke of the various elements that constituted an environment conducive to innovation—from fostering psychological safety and trust to providing the physical space and resources necessary for creative exploration. Each element, he emphasized, played a crucial role in creating a fertile ground where ideas could germinate and flourish.

With each word, Daniel underscored the importance of openness and inclusivity in their approach to creating an environment conducive to innovation. But innovation was not just about ideas, Daniel emphasized. It was also about creating a culture where every team member felt empowered to contribute their unique perspectives and talents, and where diverse voices were celebrated and valued.

With a sense of purpose and determination, Daniel challenged his team to embrace the responsibility of crafting an environment conducive to innovation—to cultivate a space where creativity could thrive, and where bold ideas were welcomed and nurtured.

And as the meeting drew to a close, Daniel and his team sat in reflective silence, surrounded by the quiet wisdom of the library's ancient tomes. For in creating an environment conducive to innovation, they had laid the foundation for a future defined by creativity, ingenuity, and collective achievement.

Encouraging Experimentation and Risk-Taking

"Embracing the Unknown: Fostering a Culture of Bold Exploration"

As the library's tranquil atmosphere enveloped them, Daniel and his executive team delved deeper into the subpoint of encouraging experimentation and risk-taking.

Surrounded by the silent guardianship of ancient tomes, the team approached this topic with a sense of anticipation, recognizing the transformative potential that came with embracing the unknown. Here, amidst the sacred halls of knowledge, they felt a stirring of excitement—a recognition of the boundless opportunities awaiting them as they ventured into uncharted territories of innovation.

Daniel, his voice a beacon of encouragement amidst the quietude, spoke of encouraging experimentation and risk-taking as the fuel that ignited the flames of creativity—the catalyst that propelled their organization towards new horizons of discovery. It was not enough to cling to the safety of the familiar, he explained. They must embrace uncertainty, stepping boldly into the realm of possibility and embracing failure as a necessary companion on the journey towards innovation.

Drawing upon the principles of "Effective Leadership, Efficient Results," Daniel spoke of the various ways to encourage experimentation and risk-taking—from providing autonomy and freedom to explore new ideas to celebrating failure as a stepping stone to success. Each approach, he emphasized, offered an opportunity to unleash the untapped potential within their teams and foster a culture where innovation thrived.

With each word, Daniel underscored the importance of courage and resilience in their approach to encouraging experimentation and risk-taking. But risk-taking was not just about blindly leaping into the unknown, Daniel emphasized. It was also about learning from failure, adapting to setbacks, and persevering in the face of adversity.

With a sense of determination and curiosity, Daniel challenged his team to embrace the spirit of experimentation and risk-taking—to cultivate a culture where bold ideas were welcomed, and where every team member felt empowered to push the boundaries of what was possible.

And as the meeting drew to a close, Daniel and his team sat in contemplative silence, surrounded by the quiet wisdom of the library's ancient tomes. For in encouraging experimentation and risk-taking, they had unlocked the door to innovation—a door that would lead them towards a future defined by bold exploration, groundbreaking discoveries, and collective achievement.

Embracing Failure as a Learning Opportunity

"Resilience in Setbacks: Lessons from the School of Failure"

As the library's timeless embrace enveloped them, Daniel and his executive team ventured into the subpoint of embracing failure as a learning opportunity.

Surrounded by the venerable tomes that whispered tales of wisdom, the team approached this topic with a mixture of trepidation and curiosity, understanding the profound lessons that lay hidden within the shadows of failure. Here, amidst the sacred sanctuary of knowledge, they felt a stirring of humility—a recognition of the transformative power of setbacks in shaping their journey towards innovation.

Daniel, his voice a gentle beacon amidst the silence, spoke of embracing failure as the alchemist's crucible—the forge where adversity was transmuted into wisdom and growth. It was not enough to fear failure, he explained. They must embrace it as an inevitable part of the journey towards innovation, and as a catalyst for deeper understanding and resilience.

Drawing upon the principles of "Effective Leadership, Efficient Results," Daniel spoke of the various ways to embrace failure as a learning opportunity—from fostering a culture of psychological safety and trust to reframing failure as a natural and necessary part of the innovation process. Each approach, he emphasized, offered an opportunity to extract valuable insights from setbacks and use them to fuel future success.

With each word, Daniel underscored the importance of

humility and resilience in their approach to embracing failure. But failure was not just about stumbling, Daniel emphasized. It was also about rising stronger and wiser, learning from mistakes, and adapting in the face of adversity.

With a sense of humility and determination, Daniel challenged his team to embrace failure as a teacher—to approach setbacks with curiosity and humility, and to extract valuable lessons from every misstep along the journey towards innovation.

And as the meeting drew to a close, Daniel and his team sat in contemplative silence, surrounded by the quiet wisdom of the library's ancient tomes. For in embracing failure as a learning opportunity, they had unlocked the door to resilience—a door that would lead them towards a future defined by growth, innovation, and collective achievement.

Recognizing and Rewarding Innovative Ideas

"Stars in the Firmament: Honoring Innovation Amidst the Night Sky"

In the tranquil embrace of the library's ancient wisdom, Daniel and his executive team ventured into the subpoint of recognizing and rewarding innovative ideas.

Surrounded by the timeless knowledge enshrined within the library's tomes, the team approached this topic with a sense of reverence and excitement, understanding the transformative impact that recognition could have on fostering a culture of innovation. Here, amidst the sacred sanctuary of knowledge, they felt a palpable energy—a recognition of the brilliance awaiting discovery within the depths of their organization.

Daniel, his voice a resonant melody amidst the quietude, spoke of recognizing and rewarding innovative ideas as the constellations that illuminated the night sky—the beacons that guided their organization towards new frontiers of possibility and discovery. It was not enough to merely acknowledge innovation in passing, he explained. They must celebrate it as the lifeblood that fueled their organization's evolution, and reward it as the precious resource that it was.

Drawing upon the principles of "Effective Leadership, Efficient Results," Daniel spoke of the various ways to recognize and reward innovative ideas—from creating awards and incentives to providing opportunities for further development and implementation. Each method, he emphasized, served to not only acknowledge individual contributions but also to inspire others to reach for the stars of creativity.

With each word, Daniel underscored the importance of celebration and appreciation in their approach to recognizing and rewarding innovation. But recognition was not just about tangible rewards, Daniel emphasized. It was also about fostering a culture where every team member felt valued and empowered to contribute their unique insights and ideas.

With a sense of excitement and gratitude, Daniel challenged his team to become champions of innovation—to seek out and celebrate the shining stars amidst the firmament of ideas, and to create a culture where creativity and ingenuity were celebrated as the cornerstones of success.

And as the meeting drew to a close, Daniel and his team sat in reflective silence, surrounded by the quiet wisdom of the library's ancient tomes. For in recognizing and rewarding innovative ideas, they had illuminated the path towards a future defined by creativity, innovation, and collective achievement.

Fostering Cross-functional Collaboration

"Bridging Horizons: Uniting Minds Across the Expanse"

In the solemn sanctum of the library, Daniel and his executive team delved into the subpoint of fostering cross-functional collaboration.

Surrounded by the timeless knowledge enshrined within the library's tomes, the team approached this topic with a sense of reverence and anticipation, understanding the transformative power that collaboration held in unlocking new realms of innovation. Here, amidst the sacred sanctuary of knowledge, they felt a stirring of camaraderie—a recognition of the untapped potential awaiting them as they united minds across the expanse of their organization.

Daniel, his voice a clarion call amidst the quietude, spoke of fostering cross-functional collaboration as the bridges that spanned the chasms between departments and disciplines—the conduits through which ideas flowed freely, and innovation thrived. It was not enough to remain siloed within their respective domains, he explained. They must break down barriers, forge connections, and cultivate a culture where diverse perspectives converged to solve complex challenges and drive collective progress.

Drawing upon the principles of "Effective Leadership, Efficient Results," Daniel spoke of the various ways to foster cross-functional collaboration—from creating interdisciplinary teams to providing platforms for knowledge sharing and idea exchange. Each approach, he emphasized, served to not only break down organizational silos but also to harness the collective intelligence of their organization in pursuit of innovation.

With each word, Daniel underscored the importance of empathy and openness in their approach to fostering collaboration. But collaboration was not just about teamwork, Daniel emphasized. It was also about creating a culture where every voice was heard, and every contribution was valued—a culture of inclusivity and respect that transcended boundaries and sparked creativity.

With a sense of unity and purpose, Daniel challenged his team to become architects of collaboration—to reach across departmental divides, build bridges of understanding, and cultivate a culture where collaboration was not just encouraged but celebrated as the lifeblood of innovation.

And as the meeting drew to a close, Daniel and his team sat in contemplative silence, surrounded by the quiet wisdom of the library's ancient tomes. For in fostering cross-functional collaboration, they had forged bonds that would transcend departmental lines, uniting their organization in pursuit of a future defined by innovation, excellence, and collective achievement.

Sustaining Innovation Over Time

"Nurturing the Flame: Sustaining the Fires of Innovation"

As the library's ambiance enveloped them in its timeless embrace, Daniel and his executive team ventured into the subpoint of sustaining innovation over time.

Surrounded by the silent sentinels of knowledge within the library's ancient tomes, the team approached this topic with a sense of solemnity and determination, understanding the delicate balance required to keep the flames of innovation burning bright. Here, amidst the sacred sanctuary of knowledge, they felt a stirring of resolve—a recognition of the responsibility that lay upon their shoulders to nurture and protect the seeds of creativity planted within their organization.

Daniel, his voice a steady beacon amidst the quietude, spoke of sustaining innovation over time as the gardener tending to the flames—the guardian of creativity tasked with ensuring its perpetual vitality. It was not enough to spark innovation in fleeting moments of inspiration, he explained. They must cultivate an environment where innovation was woven into the very fabric of their organization, where creativity was nurtured and sustained through deliberate effort and commitment.

Drawing upon the principles of "Effective Leadership, Efficient Results," Daniel spoke of the various strategies for sustaining innovation—from investing in continuous learning and development to fostering a culture of experimentation and adaptability. Each strategy, he emphasized, served to not only fuel innovation in the short term but also to lay the groundwork for its enduring legacy.

With each word, Daniel underscored the importance of perseverance and resilience in their approach to sustaining innovation. But sustainability was not just about persistence, Daniel emphasized. It was also about adaptability and foresight—a willingness to evolve and iterate in response to changing circumstances, and to cultivate a culture where innovation was celebrated as a lifelong journey, not just a destination.

With a sense of determination and commitment, Daniel challenged his team to become stewards of innovation—to tend to the fires of creativity, nurturing them through the ebb

CHAPTER SEVEN: CULTIVATING A CULTURE OF INNOVATION

and flow of time, and ensuring that they burned bright for generations to come.

And as the meeting drew to a close, Daniel and his team sat in contemplative silence, surrounded by the quiet wisdom of the library's ancient tomes. For in sustaining innovation over time, they had embarked upon a journey of legacy—a journey that would leave an indelible mark on their organization and shape the future for generations to come.

8

Chapter Eight: Leading with Emotional Intelligence

"Heartstrings of Leadership: Guiding with Emotional Intelligence"

In the serene confines of the library, Daniel and his executive team embarked on the transformative journey outlined in chapter eight: leading with emotional intelligence.

Surrounded by the profound silence of ancient tomes, the team approached this chapter with a sense of reverence and introspection, understanding the profound impact that emotional intelligence had on effective leadership. Here, amidst the sacred sanctuary of knowledge, they felt a stirring of empathy—a recognition of the interconnectedness between emotions and leadership, and the need to harness this power for positive change.

Daniel, his voice a gentle breeze amidst the stillness, spoke of leading with emotional intelligence as the conductor guiding

CHAPTER EIGHT: LEADING WITH EMOTIONAL INTELLIGENCE

an orchestra—the maestro orchestrating the delicate interplay of emotions within their organization. It was not enough to rely solely on logic and reason, he explained. They must cultivate an awareness of their own emotions and those of others, and use this insight to inspire, motivate, and empower their teams.

Drawing upon the principles of "Effective Leadership, Efficient Results," Daniel spoke of the various facets of emotional intelligence—from self-awareness and self-regulation to empathy and social skills. Each facet, he emphasized, played a crucial role in building trust, fostering collaboration, and creating a culture where every team member felt valued and supported.

With each word, Daniel underscored the importance of empathy and authenticity in their approach to leading with emotional intelligence. But emotional intelligence was not just about understanding emotions, Daniel emphasized. It was also about leveraging emotions as a source of strength and connection, and using them to navigate the complexities of human interaction with grace and wisdom.

With a sense of empathy and resolve, Daniel challenged his team to embrace the power of emotional intelligence—to cultivate a deeper understanding of themselves and others, and to lead with compassion, empathy, and authenticity in all their interactions.

And as the meeting drew to a close, Daniel and his team sat in reflective silence, surrounded by the quiet wisdom of the library's ancient tomes. For in leading with emotional intelligence, they had unlocked the key to fostering a culture of trust, collaboration, and collective success—a culture where hearts and minds worked in harmony towards a shared vision of excellence and achievement.

Understanding Emotional Intelligence (EI) and its Importance

"The Symphony Within: Harmonizing the Melodies of Emotional Intelligence"

As the library's tranquil ambiance persisted, Daniel and his executive team delved deeper into the subpoint of understanding emotional intelligence (EI) and its importance.

Surrounded by the silent guardianship of ancient tomes, the team approached this topic with a sense of reverence and curiosity, recognizing the profound impact that emotional intelligence had on effective leadership. Here, amidst the sacred sanctuary of knowledge, they felt a stirring of introspection—a recognition of the intricate interplay between emotions and leadership, and the need to cultivate this awareness for the betterment of their organization.

Daniel, his voice a soothing melody amidst the stillness, spoke of understanding emotional intelligence as the symphony that resonated within each of them—the harmonious blend of self-awareness, self-regulation, empathy, and social skills that formed the essence of effective leadership. It was not enough to merely acknowledge emotions, he explained. They must strive to understand them, harnessing their power to build connections, inspire trust, and foster collaboration within their teams.

Drawing upon the principles of "Effective Leadership, Efficient Results," Daniel spoke of the importance of emotional intelligence in navigating the complexities of human interaction and driving organizational success. He emphasized that leaders who possessed a high level of emotional intelligence were better equipped to handle challenges, resolve conflicts, and inspire their teams to achieve their full potential.

With each word, Daniel underscored the importance of empathy and authenticity in their approach to understanding emotional intelligence. He emphasized that emotional intelligence was not just a skill to be mastered but a journey of self-discovery and growth—an ongoing process of reflection and adaptation that required dedication and commitment.

With a sense of introspection and determination, Daniel challenged his team to embrace the journey of understanding emotional intelligence—to explore the depths of their own emotions, and to cultivate a deeper understanding of the emotions of others. He encouraged them to approach their leadership roles with empathy, authenticity, and a willingness to learn and grow.

And as the meeting drew to a close, Daniel and his team sat in contemplative silence, surrounded by the quiet wisdom of the library's ancient tomes. For in understanding emotional intelligence and its importance, they had taken the first step towards becoming leaders who not only inspired greatness but also nurtured the human spirit within their organization.

Developing Self-awareness as a Leader

"Reflections in the Mirror: The Journey of Self-Discovery"

As the library's timeless embrace continued, Daniel and his executive team delved into the subpoint of developing self-awareness as a leader.

Surrounded by the profound silence of ancient tomes, the team approached this topic with a sense of introspection and humility, recognizing the transformative power of self-awareness in effective leadership. Here, amidst the sacred sanctuary of knowledge, they felt a stirring of curiosity—a recognition of the journey of self-discovery that awaited them, and the profound impact it would have on their leadership journey.

Daniel, his voice a gentle whisper amidst the quietude, spoke of developing self-awareness as the journey inward—the exploration of one's thoughts, emotions, and motivations. It was not enough to simply go through the motions of leadership, he explained. They must strive to understand themselves on a deeper level, uncovering their strengths, weaknesses, and blind spots, and using this insight to become more authentic and empathetic leaders.

Drawing upon the principles of "Effective Leadership, Efficient Results," Daniel spoke of the various ways to develop self-awareness—from mindfulness practices and journaling to seeking feedback from peers and mentors. Each approach, he emphasized, offered an opportunity to peel back the layers of self-deception and cultivate a deeper understanding of oneself.

With each word, Daniel underscored the importance of humility and vulnerability in their approach to developing self-awareness. He emphasized that true self-awareness required a willingness to confront uncomfortable truths and embrace personal growth—an ongoing journey of self-discovery that required courage and commitment.

With a sense of introspection and determination, Daniel challenged his team to embark on the journey of self-awareness—to look inward with curiosity and compassion, and to cultivate a deeper understanding of themselves as leaders. He encouraged them to embrace their strengths, acknowledge their weaknesses, and strive for authenticity in all their interactions.

And as the meeting drew to a close, Daniel and his team sat in contemplative silence, surrounded by the quiet wisdom of the library's ancient tomes. For in developing self-awareness as leaders, they had taken a significant step towards becoming the kind of leaders who not only inspired greatness but also nurtured the human spirit within their organization.

Managing Emotions Effectively in the Workplace

"Navigating the Storm: Harnessing the Power of Emotional Management"

In the tranquil embrace of the library, Daniel and his executive team ventured into the subpoint of managing emotions effectively in the workplace.

Surrounded by the silent sentinels of knowledge within the ancient tomes, the team approached this topic with a mixture of anticipation and determination, understanding the critical role that emotional management played in fostering a positive work environment. Here, amidst the sacred sanctuary of knowledge, they felt a stirring of resolve—a recognition of the need to cultivate emotional intelligence to navigate the inevitable storms of the workplace.

Daniel, his voice a steady beacon amidst the quietude, spoke of managing emotions effectively as the captain steering the ship through rough seas—the steady hand guiding their organization through moments of turbulence and uncertainty. It was not enough to let emotions run unchecked, he explained. They must cultivate the ability to recognize, understand, and regulate their emotions, and to create an environment where emotions were acknowledged and managed with grace and compassion.

Drawing upon the principles of "Effective Leadership, Efficient Results," Daniel spoke of the various strategies for managing emotions effectively—from practicing mindfulness and stress management techniques to fostering open communication and conflict resolution skills. Each strategy, he emphasized, served to not only maintain harmony within the workplace but also to promote resilience and well-being among their team members.

With each word, Daniel underscored the importance of empathy and self-control in their approach to managing emotions. But emotional management was not just about keeping a stiff upper lip, Daniel emphasized. It was also about creating a culture where emotions were valued as a source of insight and connection, and where every team member felt supported in expressing themselves authentically.

With a sense of determination and compassion, Daniel challenged his team to become masters of emotional management—to cultivate a deep understanding of their own emotions and those of others, and to lead with empathy, resilience, and grace in all their interactions.

And as the meeting drew to a close, Daniel and his team sat in contemplative silence, surrounded by the quiet wisdom of the library's ancient tomes. For in managing emotions effectively in the workplace, they had unlocked the key to fostering a culture of trust, respect, and collective well-being—a culture where hearts and minds worked in harmony towards a shared vision of excellence and achievement.

Empathizing with Team Members

"Bridges of Understanding: Compassion in Leadership"

In the serene embrace of the library, Daniel and his executive team ventured into the subpoint of empathizing with team members.

Surrounded by the weighty silence of ancient tomes, the team approached this topic with a blend of reverence and compassion, recognizing the profound impact empathy had on fostering trust and camaraderie within their organization. Here, amidst the hallowed sanctuary of knowledge, they felt a stirring of empathy—a recognition of the interconnectedness between understanding and effective leadership.

Daniel, his voice a gentle echo amidst the stillness, spoke of empathizing with team members as the bridge that spanned the gap between hearts—the conduit through which understanding flowed freely, nurturing bonds of trust and respect. It was not enough to merely lead from a distance, he explained. They must strive to see the world through the eyes of their team members, to understand their joys, their struggles, and their aspirations, and to use this insight to lead with compassion and empathy.

Drawing upon the principles of "Effective Leadership, Efficient Results," Daniel spoke of the various ways to empathize with team members—from active listening and open communication to practicing perspective-taking and fostering a culture of psychological safety. Each approach, he emphasized, served to not only strengthen relationships within the team but also to promote collaboration and innovation.

With each word, Daniel underscored the importance of

humility and vulnerability in their approach to empathizing with team members. He emphasized that true empathy required a willingness to step outside of oneself, to set aside preconceptions and biases, and to embrace the humanity of others with an open heart and mind.

With a sense of empathy and connection, Daniel challenged his team to become beacons of compassion—to cultivate a deep understanding of their team members' experiences and perspectives, and to lead with kindness, empathy, and authenticity in all their interactions.

And as the meeting drew to a close, Daniel and his team sat in reflective silence, surrounded by the quiet wisdom of the library's ancient tomes. For in empathizing with team members, they had laid the foundation for a culture of trust, respect, and collective well-being—a culture where every voice was heard, and every individual felt valued and supported in their journey towards success.

Building Strong Relationships Based on Trust and Respect

"Pillars of Unity: Fortifying Bonds of Trust"

In the tranquil sanctuary of the library, Daniel and his executive team delved into the subpoint of building strong relationships based on trust and respect.

Surrounded by the ancient tomes, their pages whispering tales of wisdom, the team approached this topic with a sense of reverence and determination, recognizing the foundational importance of trust and respect in effective leadership. Here, amidst the sacred sanctuary of knowledge, they felt a stirring

CHAPTER EIGHT: LEADING WITH EMOTIONAL INTELLIGENCE

of camaraderie—a recognition of the bonds that bound them together as a team and the responsibility they bore to nurture and strengthen those bonds.

Daniel, his voice a steady beacon amidst the quietude, spoke of building strong relationships based on trust and respect as the pillars that upheld their organization—the sturdy foundation upon which all else rested. It was not enough to simply lead from a position of authority, he explained. They must earn the trust and respect of their team members through their actions, their integrity, and their commitment to their shared goals and values.

Drawing upon the principles of "Effective Leadership, Efficient Results," Daniel spoke of the various ways to build strong relationships based on trust and respect—from leading by example and demonstrating integrity to fostering open communication and accountability. Each approach, he emphasized, served to not only strengthen the bonds within the team but also to create a culture where trust and respect were valued as the cornerstones of success.

With each word, Daniel underscored the importance of authenticity and consistency in their approach to building relationships. He emphasized that trust and respect were not things that could be demanded but must be earned through their words and actions—a continuous process of building and nurturing that required patience, empathy, and a genuine commitment to the well-being of their team members.

With a sense of unity and purpose, Daniel challenged his team to become architects of trust and respect—to cultivate open and honest relationships built on mutual understanding, empathy, and integrity. He encouraged them to lead with humility and authenticity, and to foster a culture where every team member felt valued and respected for their contributions.

And as the meeting drew to a close, Daniel and his team sat in contemplative silence, surrounded by the quiet wisdom of the library's ancient tomes. For in building strong relationships based on trust and respect, they had laid the foundation for a culture of collaboration, innovation, and collective achievement—a culture where hearts and minds worked in harmony towards a shared vision of excellence and success.

Using EI to Influence and Inspire Others

"The Ripple Effect: Harnessing Emotional Intelligence for Transformation"

In the serene atmosphere of the library, Daniel and his executive team delved into the subpoint of using emotional intelligence (EI) to influence and inspire others.

Surrounded by the weighty silence of ancient tomes, the team approached this topic with a blend of curiosity and determination, recognizing the transformative power that emotional intelligence held in shaping their leadership journey. Here, amidst the hallowed sanctuary of knowledge, they felt a stirring of anticipation—a recognition of the ripple effect that their actions, guided by emotional intelligence, could have on their team and organization.

Daniel, his voice a gentle current amidst the stillness, spoke of using emotional intelligence to influence and inspire others as the pebble cast into the pond—the catalyst for waves of positive change that radiated outward, touching the lives of those around them. It was not enough to simply lead by command, he explained. They must lead by example, using their emotional intelligence to connect authentically with their team members, inspire trust and confidence, and ignite the flames of passion and purpose within them.

Drawing upon the principles of "Effective Leadership, Efficient Results," Daniel spoke of the various ways to use emotional intelligence to influence and inspire others—from practicing empathy and active listening to fostering a culture of collaboration and empowerment. Each approach, he emphasized, served to not only elevate their own leadership effectiveness but also to create a ripple effect of positivity and motivation that permeated throughout their organization.

With each word, Daniel underscored the importance of authenticity and empathy in their approach to using emotional intelligence. He emphasized that true influence and inspiration stemmed not from authority but from connection—from their ability to understand and resonate with the emotions of their team members and to lead with empathy, compassion, and integrity.

With a sense of purpose and conviction, Daniel challenged his team to become catalysts for positive change—to use their emotional intelligence to inspire greatness, foster collaboration, and create a culture where every team member felt valued, supported, and empowered to reach their full potential.

And as the meeting drew to a close, Daniel and his team sat in reflective silence, surrounded by the quiet wisdom of the library's ancient tomes. For in using emotional intelligence to influence and inspire others, they had embarked upon a journey of transformation—a journey that would ripple outward, touching the lives of all those they encountered and shaping the future of their organization for the better.

9

Chapter Nine: Optimizing Time Management and Productivity

"Navigating the Landscape of Productivity"

In the serene embrace of the library, Daniel and his executive team embarked on the transformative journey outlined in chapter nine: optimizing time management and productivity.

Surrounded by the silent sentinels of knowledge within the ancient tomes, the team approached this topic with a blend of anticipation and determination, recognizing the critical role that effective time management played in achieving their organizational goals. Here, amidst the sacred sanctuary of knowledge, they felt a stirring of purpose—a recognition of the infinite possibilities that lay before them, waiting to be unlocked through mastery of their time and resources.

Daniel, his voice a steady beacon amidst the quietude, spoke of optimizing time management and productivity as the navigator charting their course through the sands of time—

CHAPTER NINE: OPTIMIZING TIME MANAGEMENT AND PRODUCTIVITY

the guide leading their organization towards greater efficiency, effectiveness, and success. It was not enough to merely be busy, he explained. They must learn to prioritize their tasks, eliminate distractions, and focus their efforts on the activities that would yield the greatest impact.

Drawing upon the principles of "Effective Leadership, Efficient Results," Daniel spoke of the various strategies for optimizing time management and productivity—from setting clear goals and deadlines to using tools and techniques for planning and organization. Each strategy, he emphasized, served to not only maximize their individual productivity but also to create a culture of excellence and accountability within their organization.

With each word, Daniel underscored the importance of discipline and focus in their approach to time management. He emphasized that time was their most valuable resource—a finite commodity that must be invested wisely in order to achieve their organizational objectives.

With a sense of purpose and resolve, Daniel challenged his team to become stewards of their time—to embrace the principles of effective time management, prioritize their tasks with clarity and purpose, and use their time with intention and focus to drive meaningful progress towards their goals.

And as the meeting drew to a close, Daniel and his team sat in contemplative silence, surrounded by the quiet wisdom of the library's ancient tomes. For in mastering the sands of time, they had unlocked the key to unlocking their full potential and achieving their vision of success.

Setting Priorities and Managing Time Effectively

"The Sands of Prioritization: Carving Paths to Productivity"

In the tranquil sanctum of the library, Daniel and his executive team delved into the subpoint of setting priorities and managing time effectively.

Surrounded by the ancient tomes, their pages whispering tales of wisdom, the team approached this topic with a blend of anticipation and determination, recognizing the pivotal role that prioritization played in their journey towards productivity. Here, amidst the hallowed sanctuary of knowledge, they felt a stirring of purpose—a recognition of the power they held to carve paths through the sands of time and steer their organization towards success.

Daniel, his voice a steady beacon amidst the quietude, spoke of setting priorities and managing time effectively as the architects of their own destiny—the sculptors molding their days into vessels of productivity and achievement. It was not enough to simply react to the demands of the moment, he explained. They must proactively identify their most important tasks and allocate their time and resources accordingly.

Drawing upon the principles of "Effective Leadership, Efficient Results," Daniel spoke of the various strategies for setting priorities and managing time effectively—from using frameworks like the Eisenhower Matrix to categorize tasks based on urgency and importance, to leveraging time-blocking techniques to allocate dedicated time for focused work. Each strategy, he emphasized, served to not only enhance their individual productivity but also to align their efforts with the overarching goals of their organization.

With each word, Daniel underscored the importance of clarity and intentionality in their approach to prioritization. He emphasized that setting priorities was not just about making to-do lists, but about making strategic decisions about where to invest their time and energy in order to achieve their desired outcomes.

With a sense of purpose and resolve, Daniel challenged his team to become masters of their time—to embrace the discipline of setting priorities, and to use their time with intention and focus to drive meaningful progress towards their goals.

And as the meeting drew to a close, Daniel and his team sat in contemplative silence, surrounded by the quiet wisdom of the library's ancient tomes. For in setting priorities and managing time effectively, they had unlocked the key to unlocking their full potential and achieving their vision of success.

Delegating Tasks and Responsibilities

"The Dance of Delegation: Empowering Through Trust"

In the serene ambiance of the library, Daniel and his executive team ventured into the subpoint of delegating tasks and responsibilities.

Surrounded by the timeless wisdom of ancient tomes, the team approached this topic with a blend of anticipation and reflection, recognizing the pivotal role that delegation played in optimizing their collective productivity. Here, amidst the sacred sanctuary of knowledge, they felt a stirring of empowerment—a recognition of the transformative power that lay in entrusting others with responsibility.

Daniel, his voice a steady melody amidst the quietude, spoke of delegating tasks and responsibilities as the choreographer orchestrating a dance of productivity—the conductor guiding each member of the team in their unique role. It was not enough to carry the burden of tasks alone, he explained. They must learn to leverage the talents and strengths of their team members, empowering them to take ownership and excel in their areas of expertise.

Drawing upon the principles of "Effective Leadership, Efficient Results," Daniel spoke of the various strategies for delegating tasks and responsibilities—from identifying the right tasks to delegate to the right team members, to providing clear instructions and ongoing support. Each strategy, he emphasized, served to not only lighten their individual workload but also to foster a culture of collaboration and trust within their organization.

With each word, Daniel underscored the importance of trust and communication in their approach to delegation. He emphasized that effective delegation was not just about offloading tasks, but about empowering team members to grow and develop their skills, while freeing up time for leaders to focus on strategic priorities.

With a sense of empowerment and solidarity, Daniel challenged his team to embrace the art of delegation—to trust in the abilities of their colleagues, and to empower them to take ownership and initiative in their work. He encouraged them to foster an environment where delegation was seen not as a sign of weakness, but as a strategic tool for maximizing productivity and achieving collective success.

And as the meeting drew to a close, Daniel and his team sat in reflective silence, surrounded by the quiet wisdom of the library's ancient tomes. For in embracing the dance of delegation, they had unlocked the key to unlocking their full potential and achieving their vision of success, together.

Avoiding Time-Wasting Activities

"Sands of Distraction: Navigating the Tempest of Time"

In the hushed haven of the library, Daniel and his executive team delved into the subpoint of avoiding time-wasting activities.

Surrounded by the venerable volumes of wisdom, the team approached this topic with a blend of determination and vigilance, recognizing the insidious nature of distractions and their detrimental impact on productivity. Here, amidst the sacred sanctuary of knowledge, they felt a stirring of resolve—a recognition of the need to safeguard their time and attention from the siren call of time-wasters.

Daniel, his voice a firm anchor amidst the quietude, spoke of avoiding time-wasting activities as the sentinel guarding the gates of productivity—the vigilant protector of their precious resources. It was not enough to simply be aware of distractions, he explained. They must be proactive in identifying and mitigating them, creating barriers that shielded their focus from the onslaught of wasted time.

Drawing upon the principles of "Effective Leadership, Efficient Results," Daniel spoke of the various strategies for avoiding time-wasting activities—from setting boundaries around email and social media usage to using tools and techniques for time management and prioritization. Each strategy, he emphasized, served to not only reclaim their time but also to cultivate a culture of discipline and accountability within their organization.

With each word, Daniel underscored the importance of mindfulness and intentionality in their approach to avoiding time-wasting activities. He emphasized that time was their most valuable resource—a finite commodity that must be protected and invested wisely in order to achieve their goals and aspirations.

With a sense of determination and focus, Daniel challenged his team to become guardians of their time—to identify and eliminate distractions, and to use their time with intention and purpose to drive meaningful progress towards their objectives.

And as the meeting drew to a close, Daniel and his team sat in contemplative silence, surrounded by the quiet wisdom of the library's ancient tomes. For in avoiding time-wasting activities, they had reclaimed control over their time and attention, paving the way for greater productivity, effectiveness, and success.

Using Technology to Enhance Productivity

"Digital Horizons: Harnessing Technology for Productivity"

In the tranquil refuge of the library, Daniel and his executive team embarked on exploring the subpoint of using technology to enhance productivity.

Surrounded by the silent guardians of knowledge within the ancient tomes, the team approached this topic with a blend of curiosity and determination, recognizing the transformative potential of technology in optimizing their workflows. Here, amidst the sacred sanctuary of knowledge, they felt a stirring

CHAPTER NINE: OPTIMIZING TIME MANAGEMENT AND PRODUCTIVITY

of innovation—a recognition of the boundless possibilities that technology offered to streamline their processes and elevate their productivity.

Daniel, his voice a beacon amidst the quietude, spoke of using technology to enhance productivity as the navigator charting new horizons—the trailblazer leading their organization towards greater efficiency and effectiveness. It was not enough to merely embrace technology for its own sake, he explained. They must harness its power to automate routine tasks, collaborate seamlessly, and access information with unprecedented speed and accuracy.

Drawing upon the principles of "Effective Leadership, Efficient Results," Daniel spoke of the various ways to leverage technology for productivity—from adopting project management software to streamline workflows, to using communication tools for real-time collaboration, to utilizing artificial intelligence for data analysis and decision-making. Each technology, he emphasized, served to not only optimize their individual productivity but also to create a culture of innovation and adaptability within their organization.

With each word, Daniel underscored the importance of embracing technology with intentionality and foresight. He emphasized that technology was not a panacea for all productivity challenges but rather a tool to be wielded strategically, in service of their overarching goals and objectives.

With a sense of exploration and possibility, Daniel challenged his team to embrace the digital frontier—to experiment with new tools and technologies, and to leverage them to unlock new levels of efficiency and effectiveness in their work.

And as the meeting drew to a close, Daniel and his team sat in contemplative silence, surrounded by the quiet wisdom of the library's ancient tomes. For in using technology to enhance productivity, they had embarked upon a journey of innovation and discovery—a journey that would propel their organization towards new heights of success and achievement.

Implementing Time Management Techniques

"Chronicles of Efficiency: Crafting Time into Treasure"

In the tranquil expanse of the library, Daniel and his executive team journeyed into the subpoint of implementing time management techniques.

Surrounded by the venerable volumes of knowledge, the team approached this topic with a blend of determination and anticipation, recognizing the invaluable impact that effective time management could have on their productivity. Here, amidst the sacred sanctuary of wisdom, they felt a stirring of purpose—a recognition of the potential to mold their time into a precious resource, to be invested wisely in pursuit of their organizational goals.

Daniel, his voice a steady guide amidst the quietude, spoke of implementing time management techniques as the architect crafting a masterpiece—the conductor orchestrating the symphony of their days with precision and purpose. It was not enough to simply let time slip through their fingers, he explained. They must seize control of their schedules, employing proven techniques to maximize their efficiency and effectiveness.

Drawing upon the principles of "Effective Leadership, Efficient Results," Daniel spoke of the various strategies for implementing time management techniques—from utilizing the Pomodoro Technique to break tasks into manageable intervals, to employing the 80/20 rule to focus on high-impact activities, to creating daily and weekly schedules to prioritize tasks and allocate time effectively. Each technique, he emphasized, served to not only optimize their individual productivity but also to foster a culture of discipline and accountability within their organization.

With each word, Daniel underscored the importance of discipline and consistency in their approach to time management. He emphasized that time was their most precious asset—a finite resource that must be safeguarded and invested wisely in order to achieve their objectives.

With a sense of determination and purpose, Daniel challenged his team to become masters of their time—to implement time management techniques with diligence and commitment, and to use their time with intention and focus to drive meaningful progress towards their goals.

And as the meeting drew to a close, Daniel and his team sat in reflective silence, surrounded by the quiet wisdom of the library's ancient tomes. For in implementing time management techniques, they had unlocked the key to unlocking their full potential and achieving their vision of success, one well-managed moment at a time.

Balancing Work and Personal Life

"Harmony in the Hourglass: Striking the Balance"

In the serene refuge of the library, Daniel and his executive team delved into the subpoint of balancing work and personal life.

Surrounded by the timeless wisdom of ancient tomes, the team approached this topic with a blend of contemplation and resolve, recognizing the delicate equilibrium between professional obligations and personal well-being. Here, amidst the sacred sanctuary of knowledge, they felt a stirring of introspection—a recognition of the importance of nurturing both their professional and personal spheres.

Daniel, his voice a gentle melody amidst the quietude, spoke of balancing work and personal life as the conductor orchestrating a symphony—the harmonious blending of professional and personal pursuits to create a life of fulfillment and satisfaction. It was not enough to excel in one realm at the expense of the other, he explained. They must strive for balance, honoring their commitments to both their careers and their personal lives.

Drawing upon the principles of "Effective Leadership, Efficient Results," Daniel spoke of the various strategies for balancing work and personal life—from setting boundaries around work hours and commitments, to prioritizing self-care and leisure activities, to fostering open communication with colleagues and loved ones. Each strategy, he emphasized, served to not only enhance their well-being and happiness but also to cultivate resilience and effectiveness in their professional endeavors.

With each word, Daniel underscored the importance of mindfulness and intentionality in their approach to balancing work and personal life. He emphasized that true success was not measured solely by professional achievements, but by the richness and depth of their experiences in all aspects of their lives.

With a sense of determination and self-awareness, Daniel

challenged his team to prioritize their well-being and happiness—to strive for balance in their lives, and to nurture their relationships, hobbies, and passions alongside their professional pursuits.

And as the meeting drew to a close, Daniel and his team sat in reflective silence, surrounded by the quiet wisdom of the library's ancient tomes. For in balancing work and personal life, they had unlocked the key to a life of fulfillment and joy—a life where success was measured not only by career achievements but by the richness of their experiences and the depth of their connections.

10

Chapter Ten: Creating a Culture of Accountability

"Pillars of Integrity: Forging a Culture of Accountability"

In the solemn stillness of the library, Daniel and his executive team embarked on the transformative journey outlined in chapter ten: creating a culture of accountability.

Surrounded by the weighty volumes of knowledge, the team approached this topic with a blend of determination and introspection, recognizing the pivotal role that accountability played in fostering excellence and driving organizational success. Here, amidst the sacred sanctuary of wisdom, they felt a stirring of purpose—a recognition of the power they held to shape the culture of their organization through their actions and values.

Daniel, his voice a steady beacon amidst the quietude, spoke of creating a culture of accountability as the cornerstone upon which their organization would stand—the bedrock

CHAPTER TEN: CREATING A CULTURE OF ACCOUNTABILITY

of integrity and transparency upon which all else would be built. It was not enough to simply espouse the values of accountability, he explained. They must embody them in their daily actions, holding themselves and each other to the highest standards of performance and conduct.

Drawing upon the principles of "Effective Leadership, Efficient Results," Daniel spoke of the various strategies for creating a culture of accountability—from setting clear expectations and goals, to providing regular feedback and recognition, to fostering a sense of ownership and responsibility among team members. Each strategy, he emphasized, served to not only strengthen their organizational culture but also to empower individuals to take ownership of their work and contribute to the collective success.

With each word, Daniel underscored the importance of trust and transparency in their approach to accountability. He emphasized that accountability was not about assigning blame or punishment, but about creating a supportive environment where individuals felt empowered to take ownership of their actions and learn from their mistakes.

With a sense of purpose and resolve, Daniel challenged his team to become champions of accountability—to lead by example, hold themselves and each other accountable, and foster a culture where integrity, transparency, and excellence were the norm.

And as the meeting drew to a close, Daniel and his team sat in contemplative silence, surrounded by the quiet wisdom of the library's ancient tomes. For in creating a culture of accountability, they had laid the foundation for a workplace where trust flourished, performance soared, and success was not just a goal, but a way of life.

Setting Clear Expectations and Goals

"Guiding Lights: Illuminating the Path to Success"

In the sacred sanctuary of the library, Daniel and his executive team delved into the subpoint of setting clear expectations and goals.

Surrounded by the hushed reverence of ancient tomes, the team approached this topic with a blend of determination and vision, recognizing the transformative power of clarity in guiding their actions and decisions. Here, amidst the profound depths of knowledge, they felt a stirring of purpose—a recognition of the guiding lights that would lead their organization towards success.

Daniel, his voice a steady beacon amidst the quietude, spoke of setting clear expectations and goals as the guiding stars in the night sky—the luminous beacons that illuminated the path forward and steered their organization towards its desired destination. It was not enough to simply navigate by intuition, he explained. They must chart their course with precision and clarity, setting clear expectations and goals that would serve as the foundation for their collective efforts.

Drawing upon the principles of "Effective Leadership, Efficient Results," Daniel spoke of the various strategies for setting clear expectations and goals—from aligning individual objectives with organizational priorities, to communicating expectations clearly and consistently, to providing regular feedback and guidance. Each strategy, he emphasized, served to not only clarify their direction but also to empower individuals to contribute meaningfully to the achievement of their shared goals.

With each word, Daniel underscored the importance of alignment and transparency in their approach to setting expectations and goals. He emphasized that clear expectations were not just about dictating tasks, but about fostering understanding and accountability among team members, and providing them with the guidance and support they needed to succeed.

With a sense of purpose and determination, Daniel challenged his team to become architects of clarity—to set clear expectations and goals that would serve as the North Star guiding their organization towards success. He encouraged them to communicate openly and transparently, and to empower each other to strive for excellence in everything they did.

And as the meeting drew to a close, Daniel and his team sat in reflective silence, surrounded by the quiet wisdom of the library's ancient tomes. For in setting clear expectations and goals, they had illuminated the path forward, paving the way for greater alignment, accountability, and success.

Holding Yourself Accountable as a Leader

"The Mirror of Integrity: Reflections of Leadership Accountability"

In the solemn tranquility of the library, Daniel and his executive team delved into the subpoint of holding oneself accountable as a leader.

Surrounded by the venerable volumes of wisdom, the team approached this topic with a blend of introspection and determination, recognizing the profound impact of personal accountability on the culture and success of their organization.

Here, amidst the sacred sanctuary of knowledge, they felt a stirring of self-reflection—a recognition of the power they held to lead by example and inspire accountability in others.

Daniel, his voice a steady echo amidst the quietude, spoke of holding oneself accountable as the cornerstone of leadership—the mirror that reflected the integrity and commitment of a true leader. It was not enough to hold others to high standards, he explained. They must first hold themselves accountable, modeling the behavior and values they wished to instill in their team.

Drawing upon the principles of "Effective Leadership, Efficient Results," Daniel spoke of the various ways to hold oneself accountable as a leader—from taking ownership of mistakes and failures, to seeking feedback and self-improvement opportunities, to leading with integrity and transparency in all interactions. Each action, he emphasized, served to not only earn the trust and respect of their team but also to cultivate a culture of accountability and excellence within their organization.

With each word, Daniel underscored the importance of self-awareness and humility in their approach to leadership accountability. He emphasized that true accountability was not about avoiding blame or punishment, but about taking responsibility for their actions and demonstrating the courage to course-correct when needed.

With a sense of humility and resolve, Daniel challenged his team to become stewards of their own accountability—to look inward, confront their shortcomings, and strive for continuous growth and improvement in their leadership journey.

And as the meeting drew to a close, Daniel and his team sat in contemplative silence, surrounded by the quiet wisdom of the library's ancient tomes. For in holding themselves accountable as leaders, they had set a powerful example for their team, paving the way for a culture of integrity, trust, and excellence to flourish.

Establishing Accountability Systems and Processes

"Foundations of Responsibility: Building Accountability Structures"

In the sanctified ambiance of the library, Daniel and his executive team immersed themselves in the subpoint of establishing accountability systems and processes.

Surrounded by the silent sentinels of wisdom within the ancient tomes, the team approached this topic with a blend of determination and foresight, recognizing the essential role of structured accountability in fostering organizational success. Here, amidst the hallowed sanctuary of knowledge, they felt a stirring of purpose—a recognition of the need to lay sturdy foundations for accountability to thrive.

Daniel, his voice a sturdy pillar amidst the quietude, spoke of establishing accountability systems and processes as the scaffolding upon which their organization's success would be built—the framework that would uphold integrity, transparency, and excellence in all endeavors. It was not enough to rely on individual commitment alone, he explained. They must implement systematic approaches to accountability, ensuring that expectations were clear, progress was tracked, and outcomes were evaluated.

Drawing upon the principles of "Effective Leadership, Efficient Results," Daniel spoke of the various strategies for establishing accountability systems and processes—from defining roles and responsibilities clearly, to setting key performance indicators (KPIs) and milestones, to implementing regular check-ins and reviews. Each strategy, he emphasized, served to not only clarify expectations but also to empower individuals to take ownership of their work and contribute to the collective success.

With each word, Daniel underscored the importance of consistency and transparency in their approach to accountability systems and processes. He emphasized that accountability was not a one-time event but an ongoing commitment that required dedication and diligence from everyone within the organization.

With a sense of determination and vision, Daniel challenged his team to become architects of accountability—to design systems and processes that would uphold their values and drive their desired outcomes. He encouraged them to embrace accountability as a tool for growth and improvement, and to collaborate in building a culture where responsibility was not just a buzzword but a way of life.

And as the meeting drew to a close, Daniel and his team sat in contemplative silence, surrounded by the quiet wisdom of the library's ancient tomes. For in establishing accountability systems and processes, they had laid the groundwork for a resilient and thriving organization—one where trust, transparency, and excellence reigned supreme.

Providing Regular Feedback on Performance

CHAPTER TEN: CREATING A CULTURE OF ACCOUNTABILITY

"Echoes of Excellence: Nurturing Growth Through Feedback"

In the reverent atmosphere of the library, Daniel and his executive team immersed themselves in the subpoint of providing regular feedback on performance.

Surrounded by the timeless tomes of wisdom, the team approached this topic with a blend of empathy and determination, recognizing the pivotal role that constructive feedback played in fostering personal and organizational growth. Here, amidst the sacred sanctuary of knowledge, they felt a stirring of empathy—a recognition of the transformative power of feedback to guide individuals towards excellence.

Daniel, his voice a gentle cadence amidst the quietude, spoke of providing regular feedback on performance as the gentle breeze that stirred the leaves—a subtle yet powerful force that nudged individuals towards their full potential. It was not enough to offer feedback sporadically or in isolation, he explained. They must create a culture where feedback was woven into the fabric of daily interactions, a constant flow that nourished growth and improvement.

Drawing upon the principles of "Effective Leadership, Efficient Results," Daniel spoke of the various strategies for providing regular feedback on performance—from scheduling regular one-on-one meetings, to using objective metrics and benchmarks, to fostering open and honest communication. Each strategy, he emphasized, served to not only clarify expectations but also to empower individuals to take ownership of their development and contribute to the collective success.

With each word, Daniel underscored the importance of empathy and respect in their approach to providing feedback. He emphasized that feedback was not about criticism or judgment but about support and guidance—a reflection of their commitment to helping each other succeed.

With a sense of empathy and determination, Daniel challenged his team to become champions of feedback—to embrace it as a gift, both in giving and receiving, and to use it as a catalyst for growth and improvement in their personal and professional lives.

And as the meeting drew to a close, Daniel and his team sat in reflective silence, surrounded by the quiet wisdom of the library's ancient tomes. For in providing regular feedback on performance, they had planted the seeds of excellence, nurturing a culture where feedback was not just a task but a sacred duty—a gift that would continue to echo through the halls of their organization for generations to come.

Encouraging Ownership and Responsibility

"Pillars of Ownership: Empowering Through Responsibility"

In the solemn tranquility of the library, Daniel and his executive team delved into the subpoint of encouraging ownership and responsibility.

Surrounded by the weighty volumes of knowledge, the team approached this topic with a blend of determination and empowerment, recognizing the profound impact of ownership and responsibility on individual and organizational success. Here, amidst the sacred sanctuary of wisdom, they felt a stirring of purpose—a recognition of the transformative power they held to empower others and foster a culture of accountability.

Daniel, his voice a steady beacon amidst the quietude, spoke of encouraging ownership and responsibility as the

CHAPTER TEN: CREATING A CULTURE OF ACCOUNTABILITY

cornerstone of leadership—the foundation upon which their organization's success would be built. It was not enough to simply delegate tasks, he explained. They must empower individuals to take ownership of their work, fostering a sense of pride and accountability that would drive excellence and innovation.

Drawing upon the principles of "Effective Leadership, Efficient Results," Daniel spoke of the various strategies for encouraging ownership and responsibility—from empowering individuals to make decisions and solve problems autonomously, to fostering a culture of trust and empowerment, to providing opportunities for growth and development. Each strategy, he emphasized, served to not only unleash the full potential of their team but also to cultivate a culture of ownership and accountability within their organization.

With each word, Daniel underscored the importance of trust and empowerment in their approach to encouraging ownership and responsibility. He emphasized that true ownership was not given, but earned—a reflection of an individual's commitment to their work and their willingness to take ownership of their actions and decisions.

With a sense of empowerment and determination, Daniel challenged his team to become architects of ownership—to empower others to take responsibility for their work, their decisions, and their contributions to the organization's success. He encouraged them to lead by example, demonstrating a commitment to accountability and integrity in all their interactions.

And as the meeting drew to a close, Daniel and his team sat in contemplative silence, surrounded by the quiet wisdom of the library's ancient tomes. For in encouraging ownership and responsibility, they had ignited a spark of empowerment—a flame that would illuminate the path to greatness for themselves and their organization.

Celebrating Successes and Learning from Failures

"Harvest of Growth: Nurturing Success Through Reflection"

In the serene refuge of the library, Daniel and his executive team embarked on exploring the subpoint of celebrating successes and learning from failures.

Surrounded by the venerable volumes of wisdom, the team approached this topic with a blend of reflection and resilience, recognizing the profound lessons that both successes and failures held. Here, amidst the sacred sanctuary of knowledge, they felt a stirring of appreciation—a recognition of the rich tapestry of experiences that shaped their journey towards excellence.

Daniel, his voice a steady beacon amidst the quietude, spoke of celebrating successes and learning from failures as the twin pillars of growth—the fertile soil from which resilience and innovation blossomed. It was not enough to merely revel in victories or lament failures, he explained. They must embrace both as opportunities for learning and growth, cultivating a culture where every success was celebrated and every failure was met with curiosity and resolve.

Drawing upon the principles of "Effective Leadership, Efficient Results," Daniel spoke of the various strategies for celebrating successes and learning from failures—from recognizing individual and team achievements, to fostering a culture of experimentation and risk-taking, to conducting post-mortem analyses to glean insights from setbacks. Each strategy, he emphasized, served to not only reinforce positive behaviors but also to cultivate a growth mindset within their organization.

With each word, Daniel underscored the importance of resilience and reflection in their approach to celebrating successes and learning from failures. He emphasized that true growth came not from avoiding failure but from embracing it as an opportunity for growth and improvement.

With a sense of appreciation and determination, Daniel challenged his team to become stewards of their own growth—to celebrate successes with humility and gratitude, and to approach failures with resilience and curiosity. He encouraged them to foster a culture where every experience, whether positive or negative, was seen as an opportunity for learning and development.

And as the meeting drew to a close, Daniel and his team sat in contemplative silence, surrounded by the quiet wisdom of the library's ancient tomes. For in celebrating successes and learning from failures, they had sown the seeds of resilience and innovation—a harvest that would sustain them on their journey towards excellence.

Chapter Eleven: Leading Remote and Distributed Teams

"Bridging Distances: Leading Across Boundaries"

In the tranquil expanse of the library, Daniel and his executive team embarked on the enlightening chapter on leading remote and distributed teams.

Surrounded by the timeless wisdom of ancient tomes, the team approached this topic with a blend of curiosity and determination, recognizing the evolving landscape of work and the imperative to adapt to new modes of leadership. Here, amidst the sacred sanctuary of knowledge, they felt a stirring of anticipation—a recognition of the challenges and opportunities that leading remote teams presented.

Daniel, his voice a beacon of guidance amidst the quietude, spoke of leading remote and distributed teams as the navigator charting uncharted waters—the captain steering their ship through the currents of change towards the shores of success. It was not enough to simply transpose traditional leadership methods to the virtual realm, he explained. They must embrace new strategies and tools to foster collaboration, communication, and cohesion among remote team members.

Drawing upon the principles of "Effective Leadership, Efficient Results," Daniel spoke of the various strategies for leading remote and distributed teams—from leveraging technology to facilitate seamless communication and collaboration, to establishing clear expectations and goals, to nurturing a sense of belonging and camaraderie among team members. Each strategy, he emphasized, served to not only overcome the challenges of distance but also to unlock the full potential of their remote teams.

With each word, Daniel underscored the importance of empathy and adaptability in their approach to leading remote teams. He emphasized that remote leadership was not just about managing tasks but about understanding and supporting the unique needs and challenges of remote team members.

With a sense of curiosity and resolve, Daniel challenged his team to become pioneers of remote leadership—to embrace the opportunities presented by remote work, and to cultivate a culture where distance was not a barrier but an opportunity for innovation and growth.

And as the meeting drew to a close, Daniel and his team sat in contemplative silence, surrounded by the quiet wisdom of the library's ancient tomes. For in leading remote and distributed teams, they had embarked upon a journey of discovery—a journey where distance was no match for their collective determination and resilience.

Challenges and Opportunities of Remote Work

"Navigating the Virtual Terrain: Embracing Challenges, Unveiling Opportunities"

In the serene refuge of the library, Daniel and his executive team delved into the subpoint of the challenges and opportunities of remote work.

Surrounded by the venerable volumes of wisdom, the team approached this topic with a blend of introspection and determination, recognizing the seismic shift in work dynamics and the need to navigate the virtual terrain with agility and resilience. Here, amidst the sacred sanctuary of knowledge, they felt a stirring of anticipation—a recognition of the complexities and possibilities that remote work presented.

Daniel, his voice a steady beacon amidst the quietude, spoke of the challenges and opportunities of remote work as the twin peaks of a formidable mountain—the daunting obstacles that must be surmounted, and the breathtaking vistas that awaited those who dared to ascend. It was not enough to dwell on the challenges alone, he explained. They must also embrace the opportunities that remote work afforded, leveraging them to drive innovation, efficiency, and inclusivity.

Drawing upon the principles of "Effective Leadership, Efficient Results," Daniel spoke of the various challenges of remote work—from the struggle to maintain team cohesion and culture, to the difficulties of communication and collaboration across distances, to the potential for isolation and burnout among remote team members. Each challenge, he emphasized, presented an opportunity for growth and adaptation, a chance to reimagine traditional work paradigms and foster resilience in the face of adversity.

With each word, Daniel underscored the importance of empathy and creativity in their approach to remote work. He emphasized that while the challenges were real, so too were the opportunities, and it was up to them to harness the latter to overcome the former.

With a sense of determination and optimism, Daniel challenged his team to become architects of change—to embrace the challenges of remote work as catalysts for innovation and growth, and to cultivate a culture where distance was not a barrier but a springboard to new possibilities.

And as the meeting drew to a close, Daniel and his team sat in contemplative silence, surrounded by the quiet wisdom of the library's ancient tomes. For in confronting the challenges and opportunities of remote work, they had laid the groundwork for a future where distance was no longer a limitation, but a catalyst for greatness.

Building Trust in Virtual Teams

"Bridging the Divide: Fostering Trust in Virtual Connections"

In the hushed atmosphere of the library, Daniel and his executive team delved into the subpoint of building trust in virtual teams.

Surrounded by the silent guardians of knowledge within the ancient tomes, the team approached this topic with a blend of determination and empathy, recognizing the paramount importance of trust in fostering collaboration and cohesion across virtual distances. Here, amidst the sacred sanctuary of wisdom, they felt a stirring of conviction—a recognition of the need to forge bonds of trust that transcended physical boundaries.

Daniel, his voice a steady beacon amidst the quietude, spoke of building trust in virtual teams as the bridge that spanned the digital divide—the unifying force that bound individuals together in a shared purpose and vision. It was not enough to rely on face-to-face interactions, he explained. They must cultivate trust through consistent communication, transparency, and reliability, forging connections that were as strong and enduring as those formed in person.

Drawing upon the principles of "Effective Leadership, Efficient Results," Daniel spoke of the various strategies for building trust in virtual teams—from fostering open and honest communication, to demonstrating competence and reliability in remote work, to creating opportunities for team bonding and relationship-building. Each strategy, he emphasized, served to not only strengthen interpersonal connections but also to foster a sense of psychological safety and belonging among remote team members.

With each word, Daniel underscored the importance of empathy and vulnerability in their approach to building trust. He emphasized that trust was not built overnight, but through consistent effort and genuine care for one another's well-being.

With a sense of empathy and determination, Daniel challenged his team to become architects of trust—to cultivate an environment where every team member felt valued, supported, and empowered to contribute their best work. He encouraged them to lead by example, demonstrating trustworthiness in their own actions and decisions.

And as the meeting drew to a close, Daniel and his team sat

in reflective silence, surrounded by the quiet wisdom of the library's ancient tomes. For in building trust in virtual teams, they had laid the foundation for a future where distance was not a barrier but a catalyst for deeper connections and greater collaboration.

Leveraging Technology for Remote Collaboration

"Digital Frontiers: Exploring the Power of Virtual Collaboration"

In the tranquil expanse of the library, Daniel and his executive team delved into the subpoint of leveraging technology for remote collaboration.

Surrounded by the weighty volumes of knowledge, the team approached this topic with a blend of curiosity and determination, recognizing the transformative potential of technology to bridge the gaps of distance and facilitate seamless collaboration. Here, amidst the sacred sanctuary of wisdom, they felt a stirring of excitement—a recognition of the boundless possibilities that awaited them in the digital frontier.

Daniel, his voice a steady beacon amidst the quietude, spoke of leveraging technology for remote collaboration as the key that unlocked the doors of possibility—the tool that empowered them to connect, communicate, and collaborate across vast distances. It was not enough to simply rely on traditional methods of communication, he explained. They must embrace the myriad of digital tools and platforms available to them, harnessing their power to streamline workflows, facilitate real-time communication, and foster innovation.

Drawing upon the principles of "Effective Leadership, Efficient Results," Daniel spoke of the various technologies available for remote collaboration—from video conferencing and instant messaging, to project management software and virtual whiteboards, to collaborative document editing and file sharing platforms. Each technology, he emphasized, served to not only overcome the challenges of distance but also to enhance productivity, creativity, and engagement among remote team members.

With each word, Daniel underscored the importance of adaptability and experimentation in their approach to leveraging technology. He emphasized that while technology was a powerful enabler, it was their creativity and resourcefulness that would ultimately determine its effectiveness in facilitating remote collaboration.

With a sense of excitement and possibility, Daniel challenged his team to become pioneers of digital collaboration—to explore new tools and techniques, and to embrace the opportunities presented by the digital frontier.

And as the meeting drew to a close, Daniel and his team sat in contemplative silence, surrounded by the quiet wisdom of the library's ancient tomes. For in leveraging technology for remote collaboration, they had embarked upon a journey of discovery—a journey where distance was no longer a barrier, but a gateway to new horizons of possibility and innovation.

Communicating Effectively in a Virtual Environment

CHAPTER ELEVEN: LEADING REMOTE AND DISTRIBUTED TEAMS

"Voices in the Ether: Mastering the Art of Virtual Communication"

In the serene refuge of the library, Daniel and his executive team ventured into the subpoint of communicating effectively in a virtual environment.

Surrounded by the silent sentinels of knowledge within the ancient tomes, the team approached this topic with a blend of determination and adaptability, recognizing the pivotal role of communication in maintaining cohesion and clarity amidst the digital ether. Here, amidst the sacred sanctuary of wisdom, they felt a stirring of resolve—a recognition of the need to harness the power of words and technology to foster connection and understanding.

Daniel, his voice a steady beacon amidst the quietude, spoke of communicating effectively in a virtual environment as the art of weaving threads of meaning through the ether—the skillful orchestration of words and gestures to convey intent and emotion across digital channels. It was not enough to simply transmit information, he explained. They must cultivate empathy, clarity, and intentionality in their virtual communication, bridging the gap of physical distance to foster meaningful connections with their remote team members.

Drawing upon the principles of "Effective Leadership, Efficient Results," Daniel spoke of the various strategies for communicating effectively in a virtual environment—from mastering the nuances of video conferencing and nonverbal cues, to crafting concise and engaging written messages, to fostering a culture of active listening and feedback. Each strategy, he emphasized, served to not only overcome the limitations of virtual communication but also to enhance collaboration, alignment, and trust among remote team members.

With each word, Daniel underscored the importance of empathy and intentionality in their approach to virtual communication. He emphasized that while technology provided the medium, it was their ability to communicate with clarity and compassion that would ultimately determine its effectiveness in fostering connection and understanding.

With a sense of determination and empathy, Daniel challenged his team to become virtuosos of virtual communication—to embrace the opportunities presented by digital channels, and to cultivate a culture where every interaction was infused with empathy, clarity, and intentionality.

And as the meeting drew to a close, Daniel and his team sat in contemplative silence, surrounded by the quiet wisdom of the library's ancient tomes. For in mastering the art of virtual communication, they had not only transcended the barriers of distance but also forged deeper connections and stronger bonds with their remote team members.

Maintaining Team Cohesion and Morale

"Unity Beyond Borders: Nurturing Team Spirit in a Digital Age"

In the tranquil expanse of the library, Daniel and his executive team explored the subpoint of maintaining team cohesion and morale in the virtual realm.

Surrounded by the weighty volumes of knowledge, the team approached this topic with a blend of introspection and determination, recognizing the imperative to foster a sense of belonging and camaraderie among remote team members.

CHAPTER ELEVEN: LEADING REMOTE AND DISTRIBUTED TEAMS

Here, amidst the sacred sanctuary of wisdom, they felt a stirring of solidarity—a recognition of the need to transcend physical boundaries and cultivate a shared sense of purpose and identity.

Daniel, his voice a steady beacon amidst the quietude, spoke of maintaining team cohesion and morale as the bond that united them across the digital divide—the invisible thread that wove them together into a resilient and cohesive unit. It was not enough to simply connect virtually, he explained. They must create opportunities for meaningful interaction, celebration, and support, nurturing a culture where every team member felt valued, supported, and empowered to contribute their best.

Drawing upon the principles of "Effective Leadership, Efficient Results," Daniel spoke of the various strategies for maintaining team cohesion and morale—from organizing virtual team-building activities and social events, to celebrating milestones and achievements, to providing support and recognition for individual and team efforts. Each strategy, he emphasized, served to not only strengthen bonds but also to boost morale and motivation among remote team members.

With each word, Daniel underscored the importance of empathy and inclusivity in their approach to maintaining team cohesion and morale. He emphasized that while physical distance might separate them, their shared purpose and values would always unite them as a team.

With a sense of solidarity and determination, Daniel challenged his team to become champions of unity—to embrace the opportunities presented by the digital landscape, and to cultivate a culture where every team member felt connected, supported, and valued.

And as the meeting drew to a close, Daniel and his team sat in reflective silence, surrounded by the quiet wisdom of the library's ancient tomes. For in maintaining team cohesion and morale, they had not only overcome the challenges of distance but also forged deeper connections and stronger bonds that would sustain them through any challenge or adversity.

Addressing Isolation and Burnout in Remote Teams

"Bridging the Gap: Fostering Well-being in Remote Realms"

In the serene refuge of the library, Daniel and his executive team delved into the subpoint of addressing isolation and burnout in remote teams.

Surrounded by the profound wisdom of ancient tomes, the team approached this topic with a blend of empathy and urgency, recognizing the toll that isolation and burnout could take on the well-being and productivity of remote team members. Here, amidst the sacred sanctuary of knowledge, they felt a stirring of compassion—a recognition of the need to support and uplift one another through the challenges of remote work.

Daniel, his voice a beacon of guidance amidst the quietude, spoke of addressing isolation and burnout as the duty that they owed to one another—the responsibility to create a work environment where every team member felt valued, supported, and empowered to thrive. It was not enough to simply acknowledge the issue, he explained. They must actively seek solutions and implement strategies to mitigate the negative impacts of isolation and burnout, fostering a culture where well-being was prioritized alongside productivity.

Drawing upon the principles of "Effective Leadership, Efficient Results," Daniel spoke of the various strategies for addressing isolation and burnout in remote teams—from promoting work-life balance and boundary-setting, to encouraging regular breaks and time for self-care, to providing resources and support for mental health and well-being. Each strategy, he emphasized, served to not only alleviate the symptoms of isolation and burnout but also to create a supportive and nurturing environment where every team member could thrive.

With each word, Daniel underscored the importance of empathy and compassion in their approach to addressing isolation and burnout. He emphasized that while they may be physically distant, they were united in their commitment to supporting one another through the challenges of remote work.

With a sense of urgency and solidarity, Daniel challenged his team to become advocates for well-being—to actively support and uplift one another, and to create a work environment where everyone felt valued, connected, and empowered to bring their best selves to their work.

And as the meeting drew to a close, Daniel and his team sat in contemplative silence, surrounded by the quiet wisdom of the library's ancient tomes. For in addressing isolation and burnout, they had not only strengthened their bonds as a team but also demonstrated their commitment to each other's well-being and success.

12

Chapter Twelve: Conflict Resolution and Negotiation Skills

"Harmony Amidst Discord: Mastering Conflict Resolution and Negotiation"

In the serene refuge of the library, Daniel and his executive team embarked on the enlightening chapter on conflict resolution and negotiation skills.

Surrounded by the timeless wisdom of ancient tomes, the team approached this topic with a blend of curiosity and determination, recognizing the inevitability of conflict in any dynamic organization and the critical need to navigate it with skill and diplomacy. Here, amidst the sacred sanctuary of knowledge, they felt a stirring of anticipation—a recognition of the transformative power of effective conflict resolution and negotiation.

Daniel, his voice a steady beacon amidst the quietude, spoke of conflict resolution and negotiation skills as the art of finding harmony amidst discord—the skillful navigation of differing perspectives and interests to reach mutually beneficial outcomes. It was not enough to simply avoid conflict or impose one's will, he explained. They must cultivate empathy, communication, and problem-solving skills to address conflicts constructively and negotiate win-win solutions.

Drawing upon the principles of "Effective Leadership, Efficient Results," Daniel spoke of the various strategies for conflict resolution and negotiation—from active listening and empathy-building, to communication and assertiveness training, to principled negotiation and problem-solving techniques. Each strategy, he emphasized, served to not only resolve conflicts effectively but also to strengthen relationships and foster trust among team members.

With each word, Daniel underscored the importance of empathy and collaboration in their approach to conflict resolution and negotiation. He emphasized that while conflict was inevitable, it was their ability to navigate it with grace and integrity that would ultimately determine their success as leaders.

With a sense of determination and empathy, Daniel challenged his team to become masters of conflict resolution and negotiation—to embrace conflicts as opportunities for growth and learning, and to approach negotiations with integrity, creativity, and a commitment to fairness.

And as the meeting drew to a close, Daniel and his team sat in reflective silence, surrounded by the quiet wisdom of the library's ancient tomes. For in mastering conflict resolution and negotiation skills, they had not only fortified their leadership capabilities but also laid the foundation for a culture of collaboration, trust, and harmony within their organization.

Understanding the Nature of Conflict in the Workplace

"Navigating the Terrain: Exploring the Depths of Workplace Conflict"

In the tranquil expanse of the library, Daniel and his executive team delved into the subpoint of understanding the nature of conflict in the workplace.

Surrounded by the weighty volumes of knowledge, the team approached this topic with a blend of curiosity and introspection, recognizing the complexities and nuances inherent in interpersonal dynamics. Here, amidst the sacred sanctuary of wisdom, they felt a stirring of contemplation—a recognition of the need to peel back the layers of conflict to uncover its underlying causes and dynamics.

Daniel, his voice a beacon of guidance amidst the quietude, spoke of understanding the nature of conflict as the first step towards resolution—the process of illuminating the hidden forces and motivations that fueled discord and tension. It was not enough to simply address surface-level disagreements, he explained. They must delve deeper, exploring the roots of conflict to identify patterns, triggers, and opportunities for growth.

Drawing upon the principles of "Effective Leadership, Efficient Results," Daniel spoke of the various sources of conflict in the workplace—from differences in values and communication styles, to competing goals and priorities, to unresolved issues and unmet needs. Each source, he emphasized, carried its own unique challenges and opportunities for resolution, requiring empathy, insight, and strategic intervention.

With each word, Daniel underscored the importance of

empathy and curiosity in their approach to understanding conflict. He emphasized that while conflict was often perceived as negative, it also presented an opportunity for deeper understanding, growth, and transformation.

With a sense of curiosity and determination, Daniel challenged his team to become detectives of conflict—to explore its depths with open minds and compassionate hearts, and to uncover the insights and opportunities hidden within its tangled web.

And as the meeting drew to a close, Daniel and his team sat in reflective silence, surrounded by the quiet wisdom of the library's ancient tomes. For in understanding the nature of conflict, they had taken the first step towards resolution—a journey that would lead them towards greater harmony, collaboration, and success within their organization.

Strategies for Managing Conflict Constructively

"Forging Paths to Resolution: Crafting Constructive Conflict Management Strategies"

In the serene refuge of the library, Daniel and his executive team delved into the subpoint of strategies for managing conflict constructively.

Surrounded by the profound wisdom of ancient tomes, the team approached this topic with a blend of determination and pragmatism, recognizing the pivotal role of effective conflict management in fostering collaboration and harmony within the workplace. Here, amidst the sacred sanctuary of knowledge, they felt a stirring of resolve—a recognition of the need to harness conflict as a catalyst for growth and transformation.

Daniel, his voice a steady beacon amidst the quietude, spoke of strategies for managing conflict constructively as the roadmap to resolution—the deliberate navigation of differences and disagreements towards mutually beneficial outcomes. It was not enough to simply react to conflict, he explained. They must cultivate proactive approaches and tools to address conflicts as they arise, fostering communication, empathy, and collaboration in the process.

Drawing upon the principles of "Effective Leadership, Efficient Results," Daniel spoke of the various strategies for managing conflict constructively—from establishing clear communication channels and protocols for conflict resolution, to promoting active listening and empathy-building, to implementing mediation and negotiation techniques. Each strategy, he emphasized, served to not only de-escalate tensions but also to transform conflicts into opportunities for learning and growth.

With each word, Daniel underscored the importance of empathy and resilience in their approach to conflict management. He emphasized that while conflicts were inevitable, their response to them was within their control, and it was their ability to navigate conflicts with grace and integrity that would ultimately determine their success as leaders.

With a sense of determination and pragmatism, Daniel challenged his team to become architects of resolution—to embrace conflicts as opportunities for dialogue and collaboration, and to approach conflict management with creativity, compassion, and a commitment to finding common ground.

And as the meeting drew to a close, Daniel and his team sat in contemplative silence, surrounded by the quiet wisdom of the library's ancient tomes. For in crafting constructive conflict management strategies, they had not only fortified their leadership capabilities but also laid the foundation for a culture of openness, resilience, and collaboration within their organization.

Mediation Techniques for Resolving Disputes

"Harmonizing Discord: The Art of Mediation in Conflict Resolution"

In the tranquil expanse of the library, Daniel and his executive team embarked on exploring the subpoint of mediation techniques for resolving disputes.

Surrounded by the profound wisdom of ancient tomes, the team approached this topic with a blend of curiosity and determination, recognizing the transformative power of mediation in fostering understanding and reconciliation amidst conflict. Here, amidst the sacred sanctuary of knowledge, they felt a stirring of anticipation—a recognition of the potential to bridge divides and restore harmony through skillful mediation.

Daniel, his voice a beacon of guidance amidst the quietude, spoke of mediation techniques as the bridge that spanned the chasm of discord—the artful facilitation of dialogue and negotiation to reach mutually acceptable resolutions. It was not enough to simply impose solutions, he explained. They must cultivate empathy, impartiality, and creativity to guide conflicting parties towards common ground and lasting agreements.

Drawing upon the principles of "Effective Leadership, Efficient Results," Daniel spoke of the various techniques for mediation—from active listening and reframing perspectives, to facilitating constructive dialogue and brainstorming solutions, to exploring alternative dispute resolution methods such as arbitration and consensus-building. Each technique, he emphasized, served to not only resolve disputes but also to strengthen relationships and foster trust among conflicting parties.

With each word, Daniel underscored the importance of patience and perseverance in their approach to mediation. He emphasized that while conflicts may seem intractable, they often held the seeds of resolution and reconciliation, waiting to be unearthed through skillful mediation.

With a sense of empathy and determination, Daniel challenged his team to become agents of reconciliation—to embrace conflicts as opportunities for growth and understanding, and to approach mediation with compassion, creativity, and a commitment to restoring harmony.

And as the meeting drew to a close, Daniel and his team sat in reflective silence, surrounded by the quiet wisdom of the library's ancient tomes. For in mastering mediation techniques, they had not only fortified their conflict resolution skills but also reaffirmed their commitment to fostering a culture of cooperation, understanding, and respect within their organization.

Negotiation Tactics for Win-Win Outcomes

CHAPTER TWELVE: CONFLICT RESOLUTION AND NEGOTIATION SKILLS

"Forging Mutual Victories: Unveiling Negotiation Tactics for Win-Win Outcomes"

In the serene refuge of the library, Daniel and his executive team ventured into exploring the subpoint of negotiation tactics for win-win outcomes.

Surrounded by the profound wisdom of ancient tomes, the team approached this topic with a blend of determination and strategic insight, recognizing the pivotal role of negotiation in achieving mutually beneficial resolutions to conflicts. Here, amidst the sacred sanctuary of knowledge, they felt a stirring of anticipation—a recognition of the potential to turn adversarial encounters into opportunities for collaboration and growth.

Daniel, his voice a beacon of guidance amidst the quietude, spoke of negotiation tactics as the tools that unlocked the doors to win-win outcomes—the strategic maneuvers and approaches that enabled conflicting parties to find common ground and create value together. It was not enough to simply focus on one's own interests, he explained. They must cultivate empathy, creativity, and assertiveness to craft solutions that met the needs and interests of all parties involved.

Drawing upon the principles of "Effective Leadership, Efficient Results," Daniel spoke of the various tactics for negotiation—from understanding and leveraging BATNA (Best Alternative to a Negotiated Agreement), to exploring interests rather than positions, to practicing active listening and reframing, to generating options for mutual gain. Each tactic, he emphasized, served to not only expand the pie but also to build trust and rapport among negotiating parties.

With each word, Daniel underscored the importance of collaboration and integrity in their approach to negotiation.

He emphasized that while conflicts may arise from differing interests, they also presented an opportunity to create value and build stronger relationships through skillful negotiation.

With a sense of determination and strategic insight, Daniel challenged his team to become architects of mutual victories—to approach negotiation as a collaborative endeavor, and to seek solutions that not only met their own needs but also addressed the interests and concerns of others.

And as the meeting drew to a close, Daniel and his team sat in contemplative silence, surrounded by the quiet wisdom of the library's ancient tomes. For in unveiling negotiation tactics for win-win outcomes, they had not only fortified their conflict resolution skills but also reaffirmed their commitment to fostering a culture of cooperation, fairness, and mutual respect within their organization.

Building Consensus and Finding Common Ground

"Harmony Amidst Diversity: The Quest for Consensus and Common Ground"

In the tranquil expanse of the library, Daniel and his executive team embarked on exploring the subpoint of building consensus and finding common ground.

Surrounded by the profound wisdom of ancient tomes, the team approached this topic with a blend of curiosity and determination, recognizing the transformative power of consensus-building in resolving conflicts and fostering collaboration. Here, amidst the sacred sanctuary of knowledge, they felt a stirring of anticipation—a recognition of the potential to unite diverse perspectives and interests towards shared goals.

CHAPTER TWELVE: CONFLICT RESOLUTION AND NEGOTIATION SKILLS

Daniel, his voice a beacon of guidance amidst the quietude, spoke of building consensus as the art of weaving threads of agreement amidst the tapestry of diversity—the skillful navigation of differing opinions and priorities to find common ground and forge a path forward. It was not enough to simply advocate for one's own interests, he explained. They must cultivate empathy, flexibility, and diplomacy to engage stakeholders, explore alternatives, and bridge divides.

Drawing upon the principles of "Effective Leadership, Efficient Results," Daniel spoke of the various strategies for building consensus—from fostering open dialogue and information-sharing, to seeking common interests and values, to employing facilitation techniques such as brainstorming and consensus-building exercises. Each strategy, he emphasized, served to not only foster agreement but also to strengthen relationships and build trust among stakeholders.

With each word, Daniel underscored the importance of inclusivity and collaboration in their approach to building consensus. He emphasized that while conflicts may arise from differing perspectives, they also presented an opportunity to find creative solutions and build stronger partnerships through consensus-building.

With a sense of curiosity and determination, Daniel challenged his team to become architects of consensus—to embrace diversity as a source of strength, and to approach consensus-building with empathy, patience, and a commitment to finding common ground.

And as the meeting drew to a close, Daniel and his team sat in reflective silence, surrounded by the quiet wisdom of the library's ancient tomes. For in building consensus and finding common ground, they had not only fortified their conflict resolution skills but also reaffirmed their commitment to fostering a culture of collaboration, respect, and unity within their organization.

Following Up to Ensure Lasting Resolutions

"Sustaining Harmony: The Art of Follow-Up for Lasting Resolutions"

In the serene refuge of the library, Daniel and his executive team ventured into exploring the subpoint of following up to ensure lasting resolutions.

Surrounded by the profound wisdom of ancient tomes, the team approached this topic with a blend of diligence and foresight, recognizing the importance of diligent follow-up in cementing agreements and sustaining harmony. Here, amidst the sacred sanctuary of knowledge, they felt a stirring of determination—a recognition of the necessity to uphold commitments and monitor progress towards resolution.

Daniel, his voice a steady beacon amidst the quietude, spoke of follow-up as the crucial thread that wove through the fabric of conflict resolution—the conscientious oversight and support needed to ensure that agreements were honored and conflicts remained resolved. It was not enough to simply reach an agreement and move on, he explained. They must cultivate accountability, transparency, and communication to track progress, address challenges, and reinforce the commitments made.

Drawing upon the principles of "Effective Leadership, Efficient Results," Daniel spoke of the various strategies for follow-up—from establishing clear timelines and milestones, to assigning responsibilities and tracking progress, to conducting regular check-ins and evaluations. Each strategy, he emphasized, served to not only uphold agreements but also to foster trust and accountability among stakeholders.

With each word, Daniel underscored the importance of consistency and commitment in their approach to follow-up. He emphasized that while conflicts may be resolved in the moment, they also required ongoing attention and support to ensure that lasting resolutions were achieved.

With a sense of diligence and foresight, Daniel challenged his team to become stewards of resolution—to uphold the commitments made, monitor progress diligently, and address any emerging issues promptly and decisively.

And as the meeting drew to a close, Daniel and his team sat in contemplative silence, surrounded by the quiet wisdom of the library's ancient tomes. For in mastering the art of follow-up, they had not only fortified their conflict resolution skills but also reaffirmed their commitment to fostering a culture of accountability, transparency, and sustained harmony within their organization.

13

Chapter Thirteen: Ethical Leadership and Corporate Responsibility

"Guiding Light: The Essence of Ethical Leadership and Corporate Responsibility"

In the tranquil expanse of the library, Daniel and his executive team embarked on a profound journey into the realm of ethical leadership and corporate responsibility.
Surrounded by the timeless wisdom of ancient tomes, the team approached this topic with a blend of reverence and determination, recognizing the profound impact of ethical leadership on organizational culture and societal well-being. Here, amidst the sacred sanctuary of knowledge, they felt a stirring of introspection—a recognition of the imperative to lead with integrity, compassion, and a commitment to the greater good.

Daniel, his voice a beacon of moral clarity amidst the quietude, spoke of ethical leadership as the cornerstone of organizational excellence—the steadfast adherence to principles of honesty, fairness, and accountability in all endeavors. It was not enough to simply pursue profit and success, he explained. They must also consider the ethical implications of their actions and decisions, striving to create value not only for shareholders but also for society at large.

Drawing upon the principles of "Effective Leadership, Efficient Results," Daniel spoke of the various dimensions of ethical leadership—from fostering a culture of transparency and integrity, to prioritizing the well-being of stakeholders, to upholding environmental and social responsibility. Each dimension, he emphasized, served to not only build trust and credibility but also to create sustainable, long-term value for all.

With each word, Daniel underscored the importance of moral courage and ethical discernment in their approach to leadership. He emphasized that while ethical dilemmas may be complex, their commitment to doing what is right must remain unwavering.

With a sense of reverence and determination, Daniel challenged his team to become beacons of ethical leadership—to lead with integrity, compassion, and a deep sense of responsibility towards all stakeholders, and to inspire others to follow in their footsteps.

And as the meeting drew to a close, Daniel and his team sat in reflective silence, surrounded by the quiet wisdom of the library's ancient tomes. For in embracing ethical leadership and corporate responsibility, they had not only fortified their organization against ethical lapses but also reaffirmed their commitment to making a positive impact on the world around them.

Defining Ethical Leadership Principles

"The Moral Compass: Defining Ethical Leadership Principles"

Leaving the familiar confines of the library, Daniel and his executive team gathered in a serene garden, surrounded by the vibrant hues of nature's canvas, to delve deeper into the subpoint of defining ethical leadership principles.

Here, amidst the tranquility of the natural world, they felt a sense of connection to something greater—a reminder of the interconnectedness of all beings and the responsibility they bore as leaders to navigate their organization with integrity and compassion.

Daniel, his voice resonating with conviction amidst the rustle of leaves, spoke of ethical leadership principles as the guiding stars that illuminated the path forward—the fundamental values and beliefs that informed their decisions and actions. It was not enough to simply react to circumstances, he explained. They must cultivate a clear understanding of what it meant to lead ethically, grounding themselves in principles that transcended individual interests and served the greater good.

Drawing upon the principles of "Effective Leadership, Efficient Results," Daniel spoke of the core tenets of ethical leadership—from honesty and transparency, to fairness and justice, to respect for diversity and inclusion. Each principle, he emphasized, served as a compass, guiding them through the complexities of leadership and helping them navigate ethical dilemmas with clarity and integrity.

With each word, Daniel underscored the importance of moral clarity and conviction in their approach to leadership.

CHAPTER THIRTEEN: ETHICAL LEADERSHIP AND CORPORATE...

He emphasized that while ethical dilemmas may test their resolve, their commitment to upholding ethical principles must remain steadfast.

With a sense of reverence and determination, Daniel challenged his team to embrace the ethical imperative—to lead with honesty, fairness, and compassion, and to create a culture where ethical leadership was not just a lofty ideal but a lived reality.

And as the meeting drew to a close, Daniel and his team sat in contemplative silence, surrounded by the beauty of the garden's blooms. For in defining ethical leadership principles, they had not only strengthened their moral foundation but also reaffirmed their commitment to leading with integrity and purpose.

Leading by Example in Ethical Decision Making

"Walking the Talk: Leading by Example in Ethical Decision Making"

In a humble yet elegant café nestled within the heart of the city, Daniel and his executive team reconvened to explore the subpoint of leading by example in ethical decision making.

Surrounded by the comforting aroma of freshly brewed coffee and the gentle hum of conversation, they embraced the warmth of the café as a backdrop for their discussion—a reminder that ethical leadership transcended the confines of boardrooms and offices, manifesting in every interaction, large or small.

Daniel, his voice resonating with sincerity amidst the café's ambiance, spoke of leading by example as the cornerstone of ethical leadership—the commitment to align words with actions, and values with behaviors. It was not enough to simply espouse ethical principles, he explained. They must embody them in their daily lives, serving as beacons of integrity and moral courage for others to follow.

Drawing upon the principles of "Effective Leadership, Efficient Results," Daniel spoke of the importance of authenticity and consistency in ethical leadership—from honoring commitments and upholding promises, to demonstrating humility and vulnerability, to admitting mistakes and learning from them. Each action, he emphasized, spoke volumes about their character and credibility as leaders.

With each word, Daniel underscored the significance of personal integrity and accountability in their approach to decision making. He emphasized that while ethical dilemmas may be challenging, their unwavering commitment to doing what is right must guide their actions, inspiring trust and confidence in those they lead.

With a sense of resolve and authenticity, Daniel challenged his team to embrace the responsibility of leadership—to lead not only with their minds but also with their hearts, and to cultivate a culture where ethical behavior was not just a standard but a way of life.

And as the meeting drew to a close, Daniel and his team sat in companionable silence, savoring the camaraderie and connection fostered by their discussion. For in leading by example in ethical decision making, they had not only strengthened their bond as a team but also reaffirmed their collective commitment to making a positive impact on the world around them.

Promoting Diversity, Equity, and Inclusion in the Workplace

"Embracing Diversity: Fostering Equity and Inclusion in the Workplace"

Seeking a vibrant setting to explore the subpoint of promoting diversity, equity, and inclusion, Daniel and his executive team gathered in a bustling marketplace teeming with life and energy.

Surrounded by the colorful tapestry of diverse cultures and backgrounds, they felt the pulse of humanity's rich mosaic—a reminder of the importance of embracing differences and nurturing an environment where every voice could be heard and valued.

Daniel, his voice infused with passion amidst the marketplace's vibrant symphony, spoke of promoting diversity, equity, and inclusion as essential pillars of ethical leadership—the commitment to create a workplace where everyone, regardless of background or identity, could thrive and contribute to their fullest potential.

Drawing upon the principles of "Effective Leadership, Efficient Results," Daniel spoke of the importance of fostering a culture of respect and belonging—from embracing diverse perspectives and experiences, to eliminating bias and discrimination, to providing equal opportunities for growth and advancement. Each initiative, he emphasized, served to not only enrich the organization but also to create a more just and equitable society.

With each word, Daniel underscored the significance of empathy and empathy in their approach to promoting diversity and inclusion. He emphasized that while progress may be gradual, their unwavering commitment to fostering an inclusive workplace must remain steadfast.

With a sense of solidarity and determination, Daniel challenged his team to embrace the transformative power of diversity—to celebrate differences, challenge biases, and create a workplace where everyone felt valued and empowered to succeed.

And as the meeting drew to a close, Daniel and his team sat amidst the bustling marketplace, surrounded by the kaleidoscope of humanity's diversity. For in promoting diversity, equity, and inclusion, they had not only enriched their organization but also reaffirmed their commitment to building a brighter, more inclusive future for all.

Upholding Integrity and Transparency in Business Practices

"Shining Light: Upholding Integrity and Transparency in Business Practices"

In a sleek, modern conference room overlooking the city skyline, Daniel and his executive team gathered to delve into the subpoint of upholding integrity and transparency in business practices.

Surrounded by the panoramic view of the bustling metropolis, they felt the weight of responsibility inherent in their roles—the imperative to lead with integrity and ensure that their organization operated with transparency and honesty.

Daniel, his voice steady amidst the backdrop of urban energy, spoke of upholding integrity and transparency as non-negotiables in ethical leadership—the commitment to conduct business with honesty, fairness, and accountability. It was not enough to simply achieve success, he explained. They must do so in a manner that was above reproach, earning the trust and confidence of stakeholders through their actions.

Drawing upon the principles of "Effective Leadership, Efficient Results," Daniel spoke of the importance of setting high ethical standards—from adhering to legal and regulatory requirements, to promoting ethical decision making at all levels of the organization, to fostering a culture where openness and honesty were valued and rewarded. Each initiative, he emphasized, served to not only protect the organization's reputation but also to build long-term trust and credibility.

With each word, Daniel underscored the significance of personal integrity and organizational transparency in their approach to business practices. He emphasized that while the temptations of shortcuts and compromises may arise, their commitment to doing what is right must remain unwavering.

With a sense of conviction and resolve, Daniel challenged his team to embrace the responsibility of ethical leadership—to lead by example, hold themselves and others accountable, and ensure that integrity and transparency were the guiding principles of their organization's operations.

And as the meeting drew to a close, Daniel and his team sat amidst the city's bustling energy, surrounded by the glow of the skyline's lights. For in upholding integrity and transparency in business practices, they had not only fortified their organization against ethical lapses but also reaffirmed their commitment to being stewards of trust and integrity in the corporate world.

Balancing Yourself and Others Accountable to Ethical Standards

"The Ethical Balancing Act: Holding Yourself and Others Accountable"

In a serene retreat nestled within nature's embrace, Daniel and his executive team convened to explore the delicate subpoint of balancing oneself and others accountable to ethical standards.

Surrounded by the tranquil beauty of the natural world, they felt a sense of harmony and introspection—a reminder of the interconnectedness of all beings and the responsibility they bore as leaders to uphold ethical standards not only for themselves but also for those they led.

Daniel, his voice a calming presence amidst the serenity of their surroundings, spoke of the importance of balance in accountability—the need to hold oneself and others to ethical standards with fairness and compassion. It was not enough to simply enforce rules, he explained. They must also cultivate empathy and understanding, recognizing that accountability was a shared responsibility that required both support and accountability.

Drawing upon the principles of "Effective Leadership, Efficient Results," Daniel spoke of the importance of fostering a culture of mutual accountability—from leading by example and holding oneself to high ethical standards, to providing guidance and support for others to do the same, to addressing lapses in a constructive and empathetic manner. Each action, he emphasized, served to not only strengthen the ethical fabric of the organization but also to foster trust and collaboration among its members.

With each word, Daniel underscored the significance of balance and empathy in their approach to accountability. He emphasized that while accountability may sometimes require difficult conversations and decisions, it must always be grounded in fairness and understanding.

With a sense of mindfulness and compassion, Daniel challenged his team to embrace the responsibility of ethical leadership—to hold themselves and others accountable with integrity and empathy, and to create a culture where ethical standards were not just enforced but upheld with care and consideration.

And as the meeting drew to a close, Daniel and his team sat amidst the tranquility of their surroundings, surrounded by the gentle rustle of leaves and the soft chirping of birds. For in balancing oneself and others accountable to ethical standards, they had not only strengthened their organization's ethical foundation but also reaffirmed their commitment to leading with integrity and compassion.

14

Chapter Fourteen: Strategies for Personal and Professional Development

"Charting the Course: Strategies for Personal and Professional Development"

In a cozy, sunlit café nestled in the heart of the city, Daniel and his executive team gathered to explore the transformative realm of personal and professional development.

Surrounded by the comforting aroma of freshly brewed coffee and the gentle buzz of conversation, they embraced the café's warmth and hospitality as a backdrop for their discussion—a reminder that growth and learning were not confined to the boardroom but flourished in the everyday moments of life.

Daniel, his voice infused with enthusiasm amidst the café's vibrant ambiance, spoke of personal and professional development as a lifelong journey—the commitment to continuously learn, grow, and evolve as individuals and as a team. It was not enough to simply excel in their current roles, he explained. They must also invest in their personal and professional growth, acquiring new skills, knowledge, and perspectives to adapt to an ever-changing world.

Drawing upon the principles of "Effective Leadership, Efficient Results," Daniel spoke of the various strategies for personal and professional development—from setting clear goals and priorities, to seeking out mentors and coaches, to embracing challenges and opportunities for growth. Each strategy, he emphasized, served to not only enhance their individual capabilities but also to strengthen the collective resilience and agility of the team.

With each word, Daniel underscored the importance of self-awareness and commitment in their approach to development. He emphasized that while the path to growth may be challenging at times, their dedication to continuous improvement would ultimately lead to greater fulfillment and success.

With a sense of anticipation and determination, Daniel challenged his team to embrace the journey of personal and professional development—to cultivate a growth mindset, seize opportunities for learning, and support each other in achieving their full potential.

And as the meeting drew to a close, Daniel and his team sat amidst the café's inviting ambiance, surrounded by the hum of conversation and the clink of coffee cups. For in embracing strategies for personal and professional development, they had not only enriched their lives but also reaffirmed their commitment to excellence and growth, both individually and as a team.

Creating a a Personal Development Plan

"Crafting Your Path: Creating a Personal Development Plan"

Amidst the tranquil setting of a botanical garden, Daniel and his executive team reconvened to delve into the subpoint of creating a personal development plan.

Surrounded by the lush greenery and vibrant blooms, they found inspiration in the beauty and growth that surrounded them—a reminder of the potential for transformation and renewal that lay within each of them.

Daniel, his voice resonating with purpose amidst the garden's serene atmosphere, spoke of the importance of crafting a personal development plan as a roadmap for growth and achievement. It was not enough to simply aspire to greatness, he explained. They must also take intentional steps to identify their goals, assess their strengths and weaknesses, and chart a course for their personal and professional development.

Drawing upon the principles of "Effective Leadership, Efficient Results," Daniel spoke of the components of a personal development plan—from setting specific, measurable, achievable, relevant, and time-bound (SMART) goals, to identifying resources and support systems, to establishing concrete action steps and timelines. Each component, he emphasized, served to not only clarify their aspirations but also to guide their efforts and measure their progress along the way.

With each word, Daniel underscored the importance of commitment and accountability in their approach to personal development. He emphasized that while the journey may be challenging, their dedication to their growth and development would ultimately lead to greater fulfillment and success.

With a sense of purpose and determination, Daniel challenged his team to embrace the process of creating a personal development plan—to reflect on their aspirations, identify their areas for growth, and commit to taking proactive steps towards realizing their potential.

And as the meeting drew to a close, Daniel and his team sat amidst the garden's tranquil beauty, surrounded by the gentle rustle of leaves and the sweet fragrance of flowers. For in crafting their personal development plans, they had not only empowered themselves to reach new heights but also reaffirmed their commitment to continuous growth and improvement, both personally and professionally.

Continuously Learning and Growing as a Leader

"Ever Evolving: Embracing Continuous Growth as a Leader"

In a spacious, sunlit loft overlooking the city skyline, Daniel and his executive team reconvened to explore the subpoint of continuously learning and growing as a leader.

Surrounded by the panoramic view of the urban landscape, they felt a sense of possibility and potential—the reminder that growth was not a destination but a lifelong journey of discovery and evolution.

Daniel, his voice a beacon of inspiration amidst the loft's expansive ambiance, spoke of the importance of embracing continuous growth as a leader—the commitment to cultivate curiosity, adaptability, and resilience in the face of ever-changing challenges and opportunities. It was not enough to simply rest on their laurels, he explained. They must also remain open to new ideas, perspectives, and experiences, constantly pushing the boundaries of their knowledge and capabilities.

Drawing upon the principles of "Effective Leadership, Efficient Results," Daniel spoke of the various ways in which leaders could foster a culture of continuous learning and growth—from seeking out diverse sources of knowledge and expertise, to soliciting feedback and mentorship, to embracing failure as a natural part of the learning process. Each approach, he emphasized, served to not only expand their horizons but also to enhance their effectiveness and impact as leaders.

With each word, Daniel underscored the importance of humility and curiosity in their approach to continuous growth. He emphasized that while the journey may be challenging at times, their commitment to learning and development would ultimately lead to greater resilience, innovation, and success.

With a sense of enthusiasm and determination, Daniel challenged his team to embrace the mindset of lifelong learning—to approach each day as an opportunity to grow, evolve, and make a positive impact on the world around them.

And as the meeting drew to a close, Daniel and his team stood amidst the loft's panoramic vista, bathed in the golden glow of the setting sun. For in embracing continuous growth as leaders, they had not only embraced their potential for greatness but also reaffirmed their commitment to leading with purpose, passion, and excellence.

Seeking Feedback and Mentorship

"Guided by Wisdom: Seeking Feedback and Mentorship"

In the hushed ambiance of a tranquil art gallery, Daniel and his executive team gathered once more to explore the subpoint of seeking feedback and mentorship.

Surrounded by the timeless beauty of masterpieces adorning the walls, they felt a sense of reverence for the wisdom and guidance that awaited them—a reminder that growth often flourished in the presence of mentors and the feedback they provided.

Daniel, his voice a gentle cadence amidst the gallery's serene atmosphere, spoke of the importance of seeking feedback and mentorship as essential components of personal and professional development. It was not enough to navigate the complexities of leadership alone, he explained. They must also humbly seek the insights and perspectives of others, drawing upon their wisdom and experience to inform their own growth and learning.

Drawing upon the principles of "Effective Leadership, Efficient Results," Daniel spoke of the transformative power of feedback and mentorship—from soliciting input from peers, colleagues, and subordinates, to seeking out mentors who could offer guidance and support, to embracing constructive criticism as a catalyst for growth. Each approach, he emphasized, served to not only broaden their perspectives but also to deepen their self-awareness and effectiveness as leaders.

With each word, Daniel underscored the importance of humility and openness in their approach to seeking feedback and mentorship. He emphasized that while the journey may be humbling at times, their willingness to learn from others would ultimately lead to greater insight, resilience, and success.

With a sense of gratitude and anticipation, Daniel challenged his team to embrace the opportunity to seek feedback and mentorship—to approach each interaction as a chance to learn, grow, and become better leaders.

And as the meeting drew to a close, Daniel and his team stood amidst the gallery's quiet splendor, surrounded by the timeless wisdom of the artworks that surrounded them. For in seeking feedback and mentorship, they had not only honored the legacy of those who came before them but also reaffirmed their commitment to continuous growth and excellence, both personally and professionally.

Networking and Building Professional Relationships

"Connections That Count: Networking and Building Professional Relationships"

Amidst the lively atmosphere of a bustling networking event, Daniel and his executive team gathered to explore the subpoint of networking and building professional relationships.

Surrounded by the energetic buzz of conversation and the clinking of glasses, they felt the pulse of opportunity and connection that permeated the air—a reminder that relationships were the cornerstone of success in the modern workplace.

Daniel, his voice animated amidst the event's vibrant ambiance, spoke of the importance of networking and building professional relationships as essential elements of personal and professional growth. It was not enough to excel in isolation, he explained. They must also cultivate a robust network of contacts and collaborators, drawing upon the collective wisdom and support of their professional community to propel them forward.

Drawing upon the principles of "Effective Leadership, Efficient Results," Daniel spoke of the various strategies for networking and relationship-building—from attending industry events and conferences, to participating in professional associations and clubs, to leveraging social media and online platforms to connect with like-minded individuals. Each strategy, he emphasized, served to not only expand their sphere of influence but also to foster collaboration, innovation, and opportunity.

With each word, Daniel underscored the importance of authenticity and reciprocity in their approach to networking. He emphasized that while the landscape of networking may be vast and dynamic, their commitment to building genuine, mutually beneficial relationships would ultimately lead to greater success and fulfillment.

With a sense of excitement and camaraderie, Daniel challenged his team to embrace the power of networking and relationship-building—to seize every opportunity to connect with others, share their knowledge and expertise, and forge meaningful connections that could enrich their professional lives.

And as the event drew to a close, Daniel and his team mingled amidst the crowd, surrounded by the hum of conversation and the warmth of newfound connections. For in networking and building professional relationships, they had not only expanded their horizons but also reaffirmed their commitment to growth, collaboration, and success in the modern workplace.

Balancing Ambition with Self-care

"Harmony in Pursuit: Balancing Ambition with Self-care"

In the serene tranquility of a wellness retreat nestled amidst nature's embrace, Daniel and his executive team gathered to explore the delicate subpoint of balancing ambition with self-care.

Surrounded by the gentle rustle of leaves and the soothing melody of birdsong, they felt a sense of peace and rejuvenation wash over them—a reminder that success was not just about achieving goals but also about nurturing their well-being along the way.

Daniel, his voice a calming presence amidst the retreat's tranquil ambiance, spoke of the importance of balancing ambition with self-care as essential for sustaining long-term success and fulfillment. It was not enough to relentlessly pursue goals, he explained. They must also prioritize their physical, mental, and emotional well-being, cultivating a sense of harmony and balance in their lives.

Drawing upon the principles of "Effective Leadership, Efficient Results," Daniel spoke of the various strategies for balancing ambition with self-care—from setting boundaries and managing workload, to practicing mindfulness and stress management techniques, to prioritizing rest, relaxation, and leisure activities. Each strategy, he emphasized, served to not only prevent burnout and exhaustion but also to enhance their resilience, creativity, and effectiveness as leaders.

With each word, Daniel underscored the importance of self-awareness and intentionality in their approach to balancing ambition with self-care. He emphasized that while the pursuit of excellence may be all-consuming at times, their commitment to nurturing their well-being would ultimately lead to greater vitality, joy, and fulfillment in both their personal and professional lives.

With a sense of serenity and purpose, Daniel challenged his team to embrace the practice of self-care—to honor their needs, prioritize their health and happiness, and create space for rest, reflection, and rejuvenation amidst the demands of their ambitious goals.

And as the retreat drew to a close, Daniel and his team basked in the glow of the setting sun, surrounded by the gentle beauty of nature's embrace. For in balancing ambition with self-care, they had not only honored their commitment to excellence but also reaffirmed their dedication to living fully and authentically, both as leaders and as individuals.

Reflecting on Your Leadership Journey

"Journey of Reflection: Navigating Your Leadership Path"

In the quiet solitude of a tranquil mountain retreat, Daniel and his executive team gathered to explore the introspective subpoint of reflecting on their leadership journey.

Surrounded by the majestic beauty of towering peaks and cascading waterfalls, they felt a sense of awe and reverence for the journey they had embarked upon—a reminder that leadership was not just about reaching destinations but also about embracing the transformative power of self-reflection along the way.

Daniel, his voice a gentle echo amidst the mountain's serene embrace, spoke of the importance of reflecting on one's leadership journey as a means of gaining insight, clarity, and wisdom. It was not enough to simply forge ahead, he explained. They must also take time to pause, look back, and ponder the lessons learned, the challenges overcome, and the growth experienced along the way.

Drawing upon the principles of "Effective Leadership, Efficient Results," Daniel spoke of the various ways in which leaders could engage in reflective practice—from journaling and meditation, to seeking feedback and mentorship, to participating in leadership development programs and retreats. Each approach, he emphasized, served to not only deepen their self-awareness but also to inform their future actions and decisions as leaders.

With each word, Daniel underscored the importance of humility and curiosity in their approach to reflection. He emphasized that while the path of leadership may be winding and uncertain, their commitment to self-discovery and growth would ultimately lead to greater insight, resilience, and effectiveness.

With a sense of reverence and contemplation, Daniel challenged his team to embrace the practice of reflection—to set aside time for quiet introspection, to honor their experiences and insights, and to use their reflections as a compass for navigating their leadership journey with purpose and intention.

And as the retreat drew to a close, Daniel and his team stood amidst the mountain's timeless beauty, surrounded by the whispers of the wind and the gentle rustle of leaves. For in reflecting on their leadership journey, they had not only honored their past but also reaffirmed their commitment to leading with authenticity, wisdom, and grace in the days and years to come.

15

Chapter Fifteen: Sustaining Leadership Excellence

"The Legacy of Leadership: Sustaining Excellence"

In the stately elegance of a historic mansion, Daniel and his executive team gathered one final time to explore the culminating chapter of their journey: sustaining leadership excellence.

Surrounded by the grandeur of polished marble floors and ornate chandeliers, they felt a sense of gravity and reverence for the responsibility they bore as stewards of their organization's legacy—a reminder that leadership was not just about achieving success but also about preserving and perpetuating excellence for generations to come.

Daniel, his voice resonating with conviction amidst the mansion's dignified ambiance, spoke of the importance of sustaining leadership excellence as the final act of their leadership journey. It was not enough to simply achieve greatness, he explained. They must also commit to upholding and advancing the standards of excellence they had worked so hard to establish.

Drawing upon the principles of "Effective Leadership, Efficient Results," Daniel spoke of the various strategies for sustaining leadership excellence—from fostering a culture of continuous improvement and innovation, to investing in leadership development and succession planning, to embracing change and adaptation as necessary to stay ahead in a rapidly evolving world. Each strategy, he emphasized, served to not only preserve their organization's legacy but also to ensure its continued relevance and success in the years to come.

With each word, Daniel underscored the importance of perseverance and foresight in their approach to sustaining excellence. He emphasized that while the road ahead may be fraught with challenges and uncertainties, their commitment to leadership excellence would ultimately serve as a beacon of inspiration and guidance for those who followed in their footsteps.

With a sense of solemnity and determination, Daniel challenged his team to embrace the responsibility of sustaining leadership excellence—to honor the past, seize the present, and shape the future with wisdom, integrity, and vision.

And as the gathering drew to a close, Daniel and his team stood amidst the mansion's timeless splendor, surrounded by the echoes of history and the promise of tomorrow. For in sustaining leadership excellence, they had not only fulfilled their duty as leaders but also left an indelible mark on the world—a legacy of excellence that would endure for generations to come.

CHAPTER FIFTEEN: SUSTAINING LEADERSHIP EXCELLENCE

Staying Agile and Adaptable in a Changing Landscape

"Navigating the Tides: Staying Agile in a Changing Landscape"

As the sun began to set over the horizon, casting a warm glow over the horizon, Daniel and his executive team remained in deep discussion, exploring the critical subpoint of staying agile and adaptable in a changing landscape.

Amidst the elegant surroundings of the mansion, with its walls adorned with portraits of past leaders and its halls echoing with the whispers of history, they felt the weight of their responsibility to navigate the uncertain waters of the future—a reminder that leadership was not just about standing firm in the face of adversity but also about embracing change with courage and resilience.

Daniel, his voice steady amidst the gathering twilight, spoke of the importance of staying agile and adaptable as essential qualities of effective leadership. It was not enough to cling to the familiar, he explained. They must also be willing to embrace change, to pivot when necessary, and to chart a new course in response to the shifting currents of the world around them.

Drawing upon the principles of "Effective Leadership, Efficient Results," Daniel spoke of the various strategies for staying agile and adaptable—from fostering a culture of innovation and experimentation, to empowering teams to take calculated risks, to embracing failure as a natural part of the learning process. Each strategy, he emphasized, served to not only enhance their organization's resilience but also to position it for success in an ever-changing landscape.

With each word, Daniel underscored the importance of flexibility and foresight in their approach to staying agile. He emphasized that while the journey ahead may be fraught with uncertainty, their willingness to adapt and evolve would ultimately lead to greater strength, vitality, and relevance in the face of adversity.

With a sense of determination and resolve, Daniel challenged his team to embrace the challenge of staying agile and adaptable—to view change not as a threat but as an opportunity for growth, innovation, and renewal.

And as the last rays of sunlight faded into the darkness of night, Daniel and his team stood together in silent contemplation, surrounded by the timeless grandeur of the mansion and the promise of a new dawn. For in staying agile and adaptable, they had not only honored the legacy of those who came before them but also forged a path forward into the unknown—a path illuminated by the light of their courage, resilience, and unwavering commitment to excellence.

Mentoring the Next Generation of Leaders

"Passing the Torch: Mentoring the Leaders of Tomorrow"

As the evening deepened and the shadows lengthened, Daniel and his executive team shifted their focus to the crucial subpoint of mentoring the next generation of leaders.

Within the opulent halls of the mansion, where the air was tinged with the scent of aged wood and polished brass, they felt a profound sense of duty and privilege—a reminder that leadership was not just about achieving personal success but also about investing in the growth and development of those

CHAPTER FIFTEEN: SUSTAINING LEADERSHIP EXCELLENCE

who would carry the torch forward into the future.

Daniel, his voice resonant with authority amidst the mansion's dignified surroundings, spoke of the importance of mentoring as a cornerstone of leadership excellence. It was not enough to simply lead, he explained. They must also nurture and guide the next generation, imparting their wisdom and experience to prepare them for the challenges and opportunities that lay ahead.

Drawing upon the principles of "Effective Leadership, Efficient Results," Daniel spoke of the various ways in which leaders could mentor the next generation—from providing coaching and feedback, to offering opportunities for growth and development, to serving as role models and sources of inspiration. Each approach, he emphasized, served to not only empower future leaders but also to strengthen the fabric of their organization and ensure its continued success in the years to come.

With each word, Daniel underscored the importance of generosity and humility in their approach to mentoring. He emphasized that while the act of passing on knowledge and experience may be humbling, their investment in the growth and development of others would ultimately serve as their greatest legacy.

With a sense of purpose and commitment, Daniel challenged his team to embrace the responsibility of mentoring the next generation of leaders—to share their knowledge, support their growth, and empower them to reach their full potential.

And as the evening wore on and the moon rose high in the sky, Daniel and his team lingered in the mansion's hallowed halls, surrounded by the echoes of the past and the promise of the future. For in mentoring the leaders of tomorrow, they had not only honored their duty as stewards of their organization but also ensured that their legacy of excellence would endure for generations to come.

Leading by Example in Continuous Improvement

"A Legacy of Growth: Leading by Example in Continuous Improvement"

As the night grew deeper, Daniel and his executive team delved into the vital subpoint of leading by example in continuous improvement.

Within the regal atmosphere of the mansion, where the air was thick with the scent of old books and the soft glow of candlelight illuminated the room, they felt a profound sense of duty and inspiration—a reminder that leadership was not just about achieving greatness, but also about demonstrating a commitment to lifelong learning and growth.

Daniel, his voice infused with conviction amidst the mansion's timeless ambiance, spoke of the importance of leading by example in continuous improvement as a hallmark of effective leadership. It was not enough to rest on past achievements, he explained. They must also embrace a mindset of constant evolution and refinement, inspiring others to follow suit.

Drawing upon the principles of "Effective Leadership, Efficient Results," Daniel spoke of the various ways in which leaders could lead by example in continuous improvement—from setting ambitious goals and challenging the status quo, to seeking out feedback and actively seeking opportunities for development, to demonstrating resilience and adaptability in the face of adversity. Each approach, he emphasized, served to not only elevate their own leadership but also to inspire those around them to strive for excellence.

With each word, Daniel underscored the importance of humility and self-awareness in their approach to continuous improvement. He emphasized that while the journey of growth may be challenging at times, their commitment to leading by example would ultimately serve as a beacon of inspiration and guidance for others.

With a sense of determination and purpose, Daniel challenged his team to embrace the ethos of continuous improvement—to commit themselves to the pursuit of excellence, to lead by example in their own growth and development, and to inspire those around them to do the same.

And as the night deepened and the stars twinkled overhead, Daniel and his team lingered in the mansion's grandeur, surrounded by the weight of their responsibility and the promise of their potential. For in leading by example in continuous improvement, they had not only honored their commitment to excellence, but also paved the way for a future filled with growth, innovation, and success.

Leveraging Feedback for Ongoing Growth

"Feedback: The Fuel for Growth"

In the quiet hours of the night, Daniel and his executive team embarked on the essential subpoint of leveraging feedback for ongoing growth.

Within the dignified chambers of the mansion, where the flickering candlelight cast dancing shadows on the walls adorned with portraits of past leaders, they felt a sense of reverence for the transformative power of feedback—a reminder that leadership was not just about receiving praise, but also about embracing constructive criticism as a catalyst for improvement.

Daniel, his voice a beacon of wisdom amidst the hushed atmosphere of the mansion, spoke of the importance of leveraging feedback as a cornerstone of continuous growth. It was not enough to seek validation, he explained. They must also actively solicit feedback from others, welcoming diverse perspectives and insights to inform their ongoing development as leaders.

Drawing upon the principles of "Effective Leadership, Efficient Results," Daniel spoke of the various ways in which leaders could leverage feedback for ongoing growth—from creating a culture of openness and transparency where feedback was freely given and received, to actively seeking out feedback from peers, colleagues, and subordinates, to using feedback as a springboard for reflection, learning, and improvement. Each approach, he emphasized, served to not only enhance their self-awareness and effectiveness as leaders, but also to foster a culture of continuous improvement within their organization.

With each word, Daniel underscored the importance of humility and courage in their approach to leveraging feedback. He emphasized that while the process of receiving feedback may be uncomfortable at times, their willingness to embrace it with an open mind and a growth mindset would ultimately lead to greater insight, resilience, and effectiveness as leaders.

With a sense of purpose and determination, Daniel challenged his team to embrace feedback as a gift—to view it not as a critique of their shortcomings, but as an opportunity for growth and development, both personally and professionally.

And as the night wore on and the moon cast its silvery light upon the mansion's grandeur, Daniel and his team remained in deep discussion, surrounded by the echoes of history and the promise of their potential. For in leveraging feedback for ongoing growth, they had not only honored their commitment to excellence, but also laid the foundation for a future filled with growth, innovation, and success.

Cultivating a Culture of Learning and Development

"Nurturing Growth: Cultivating a Culture of Learning and Development"

As the night deepened, Daniel and his executive team delved into the pivotal subpoint of cultivating a culture of learning and development.

Within the regal confines of the mansion, where the flickering candlelight cast a warm glow upon the ancient walls adorned with portraits of esteemed predecessors, they felt a profound sense of responsibility and possibility—a reminder that leadership was not just about individual achievement, but also about fostering an environment where every member could thrive and grow.

Daniel, his voice resonating with passion amidst the quiet elegance of the mansion, spoke of the importance of cultivating a culture of learning and development as the cornerstone of organizational success. It was not enough to focus solely on results, he explained. They must also prioritize the growth and development of their people, creating a community where curiosity was celebrated, and innovation flourished.

Drawing upon the principles of "Effective Leadership, Efficient Results," Daniel spoke of the various ways in which leaders could cultivate a culture of learning and development—from investing in training and professional development programs, to providing opportunities for mentorship and coaching, to fostering a mindset of continuous improvement and adaptation. Each approach, he emphasized, served to not only enhance individual capabilities but also to strengthen the collective resilience and agility of the organization as a whole.

With each word, Daniel underscored the importance of empowerment and inclusivity in their approach to cultivating a culture of learning and development. He emphasized that while the journey of growth may be challenging at times, their commitment to creating an environment where every member could thrive and reach their full potential would ultimately lead to greater innovation, collaboration, and success.

With a sense of determination and purpose, Daniel challenged his team to embrace their role as stewards of learning and development—to foster an atmosphere where curiosity was encouraged, feedback was valued, and every member felt empowered to contribute their unique talents and perspectives to the organization's collective growth.

And as the night wore on and the candles burned low, Daniel and his team remained in deep conversation, surrounded by the echoes of their shared vision and the promise of a brighter future. For in cultivating a culture of learning and development, they had not only honored their commitment to excellence, but also laid the groundwork for a legacy of innovation, resilience, and enduring success.

CHAPTER FIFTEEN: SUSTAINING LEADERSHIP EXCELLENCE

Leaving a Lasting Legacy as a Leader

"Legacy of Leadership: A Lasting Impression"

In the quiet stillness of the night, Daniel and his executive team approached the final subpoint of their discussion: leaving a lasting legacy as a leader.

Within the walls of the mansion, where the flickering candlelight cast soft shadows on the ornate furnishings and the air was thick with the weight of history, they felt a sense of reverence and reflection—a reminder that leadership was not just about achieving success in the present, but also about shaping the future with purpose and vision.

Daniel, his voice carrying a tone of solemnity amidst the tranquil atmosphere of the mansion, spoke of the importance of leaving a lasting legacy as the culmination of their leadership journey. It was not enough to focus solely on their own accomplishments, he explained. They must also consider the impact they would leave behind—a legacy that would endure long after they had passed the torch to the next generation of leaders.

Drawing upon the principles of "Effective Leadership, Efficient Results," Daniel spoke of the various ways in which leaders could leave a lasting legacy—from building a culture of excellence and integrity, to empowering others to succeed and grow, to making a positive impact on the lives of those they served. Each action, he emphasized, had the potential to leave an indelible mark on the organization and the world beyond.

With each word, Daniel underscored the importance of purpose and intentionality in their approach to leaving a lasting legacy. He emphasized that while the path to leadership excellence may be challenging, their commitment to making a meaningful difference would ultimately define their legacy and shape the future of their organization for generations to come.

With a sense of reverence and resolve, Daniel challenged his team to embrace the opportunity to leave a lasting legacy—to reflect on their values, their actions, and their impact, and to consider how they could make a positive difference in the world around them.

And as the night drew to a close and the candles burned low, Daniel and his team stood together in silent contemplation, surrounded by the echoes of their shared purpose and the promise of their potential. For in leaving a lasting legacy as leaders, they had not only honored their commitment to excellence, but also paved the way for a future filled with hope, inspiration, and enduring success.

About the Author

Goodson Mumba is a multifaceted individual known for his diverse expertise and prolific contributions across various fields. As an infopreneur, Management, thought leader, and spiritual leader, he has inspired countless individuals through his insightful teachings and impactful writings. Mumba is also an accomplished author, with several notable works to his name, including "Understanding Corporate Worship," "The Years I Spent in a Week," "Management By Harmony," "The CEO's Diary," "Change to Change" and "Creative Thinking for results" His literary works span topics ranging from business management to personal development and spirituality, reflecting his broad range of interests and insights.

With a Master of Business Leadership (MBL) and a Bachelor of Arts in Theology (BTh), Mumba brings a unique blend of business acumen and spiritual wisdom to his work. His educational background is further enriched by a Group Diploma in Management Studies, providing him with a solid foundation in organizational dynamics and leadership principles. Additionally, Mumba holds diplomas in Education Psychology,

Leadership and Management Styles, Organizational Behaviour, Financial Accounting, Economic Growth and Development, and Project Management, showcasing his commitment to continuous learning and professional development.

Mumba's expertise extends beyond traditional academic disciplines, encompassing areas such as Neuro-Linguistic Programming (NLP) and Positive Psychology. His diverse skill set is complemented by a range of certifications, including Creative Problem Solving and Decision Making, Life Coaching Fundamentals and Techniques, Professional Life Coaching, and Performance Management System Design. These certifications reflect Mumba's dedication to equipping himself with the tools and knowledge necessary to empower others and drive positive change.

As an author, Mumba's writings reflect his deep understanding of human nature, organizational dynamics, and spiritual principles. His works offer practical insights, actionable strategies, and inspirational guidance for individuals seeking personal growth, professional success, and spiritual fulfillment. Mumba's holistic approach to life and leadership resonates with readers worldwide, making him a respected figure in both the business and spiritual communities.

Overall, Goodson Mumba's diverse background, extensive knowledge, and profound insights make him a sought-after speaker, mentor, and author. His commitment to excellence, lifelong learning, and service to others continues to inspire individuals to unlock their full potential and lead lives of purpose and significance.

Goodson Mumba is renowned for initiating the concept of Management by Harmony, revolutionizing traditional management practices with a focus on balanced and holistic approaches. He has authored two influential books on this subject: "Introduction to Management by Harmony" and its sequel, "Management by Harmony."

Mumba's work has significantly impacted the field, offering innovative strategies for fostering organizational harmony and efficiency. His contributions continue to shape contemporary management theories and practices.

www.ingramcontent.com/pod-product-compliance
Lightning Source LLC
Chambersburg PA
CBHW052253220526
45471CB00001B/313